QUEER COMMUNION

Queer Communion

RELIGION IN APPALACHIA

Edited by
DAVIS SHOULDERS

Foreword by
WILLIE EDWARD TAYLOR CARVER JR.

Scholarly publisher for the Commonwealth, serving Bellarmine University, Berea College, Centre College of Kentucky, Eastern Kentucky University, The Filson Historical Society, Georgetown College, Kentucky Historical Society, Kentucky State University, Morehead State University, Murray State University, Northern Kentucky University, Spalding University, Transylvania University, University of Kentucky, University of Louisville, University of Pikeville, and Western Kentucky University.

Editorial and Sales Offices: The University Press of Kentucky
663 South Limestone Street, Lexington, Kentucky 40508-4008
www.kentuckypress.com

Cataloging-in-Publication data available from the Library of Congress

ISBN 978-1-9859-0295-4 (hardcover)
ISBN 978-1-9859-0296-1 (paperback)
ISBN 978-1-9859-0298-5 (pdf)
ISBN 978-1-9859-0297-8 (epub)

Member of the Association
of University Presses

To the Queer Appalachians I've shared communion with . . .

. . . and to those yet to come.

CONTENTS

Foreword

WILLIE EDWARD TAYLOR CARVER JR.

Last week, I watched a debut screening of the Flannery O'Connor biopic film *Wildcat* with my husband. During an emotionally charged moment, a bedridden Flannery, speaking with a priest, alludes to her desire for her life's work and faith to be meaningful and real, unlike the thoughtless rituals of those around her, including her mother. I can't pretend to remember exactly what she said, because as Flannery sobs in fear of being like those around her, the scene shifts to show her mother, Regina Cline, a woman long considered to be the inspiration for some of Flannery's less-than-flattering characters, listening and crying alone outside the room. But she wasn't alone. There beside me, pulling me from the film, was my husband weeping with Regina in a show of his deep empathy for what must have been a lifetime of feeling judged by her brilliant and misunderstood daughter.

As I sat ignoring the movie and carefully watching my husband remove his glasses and wipe away tears with the end of his sleeve, I thought about how strange it should be that he should expend any energy on Regina. She was a conservative Catholic woman in the early 1960s in good social standing in her small town in south Georgia. I can only guess what she would have thought of any gay man, even the tenderhearted one weeping alongside her nearly thirty years after her death. A part of me, if I am perfectly honest, was even slightly frustrated at the thought that there are gay men who weep over conservative women who probably hate us.

But I didn't hold onto that feeling for long.

It occurred to me, gay Appalachian man that I am, that effectively *all* rural queer Appalachians and Southerners have loved people who hated them—or at least parts of them, parts that can't be divided out. If we hadn't loved people who hated parts of us, many—perhaps even most—of us would never have learned to feel love at all.

That realization made me immediately think of *Queer Communion* and the stories of so many queer Appalachians who manage not only to find truth in the universe after being raised in a world that condemns them but also to find holiness in it.

There is holiness in my husband weeping for Regina, in his concern for the emotional anguish of folks who, in their quest to find God, so often do not extend that concern to us. There is holiness in his seeing in her the women in his past with whom his relationships were just as painful, as misunderstood across time and space, as heartbreaking.

I, too, love people who hate parts of me that can't be divided out.

I was raised in a right-wing evangelical church so small it became an extension of my family. Many of my aunts taught Sunday school over the years. My uncles preached. My cousins wept and had hands laid on them during altar calls while my mother sang music and her sisters played guitar. Church was God and church was family and family was church and I was family—but as a kid who knew he was gay before he even knew other churches existed, I knew I didn't really belong to church or God.

Just in case I hadn't realized it, they made sure to let me know. The same uncles who called me fag and gay and mocked how I moved and spoke like a sissy preached the sermons declaring that all fags and gays and sissies were going to hell. Those same aunts whose sweet melodies coaxed the broken to Christ used their voices to tell me I was strange, that I acted like a girl, that I should feel shame. Those same cousins who wept under loving hands hoping to feel God were among my first and worst bullies.

But I loved them all.

The same aunts who reminded me of my inadequacy also fed me my favorite foods, checked in on us when our mom was sick, and bought Christmas presents when money was tight. Those same uncles would make me laugh when I wanted to cry. Those cousins who mocked me were also the first to defend me when someone else did it.

To this day, when somebody cracks a joke about rednecks or hillbillies, I know they picture some of my family members: folks in the hills trying to get by. I defend them because it breaks my heart that someone can't see how intelligent they are. It breaks my heart that someone can't see how hardworking they are. It breaks my heart that someone can't see how resourceful they are. And, honestly, it breaks my heart because I love them.

Love is, over and over again, what the speakers in *Queer Communion* seek to create and find. It is the lens the spirit needs to witness truth lurking behind the brokenness of this world. Love is found in an unwelcoming home, in grandmothers who never knew all the parts of us, in taking back symbols and rediscovering them in new contexts, in art, in dancing with someone, in song, in the present moment, and in growing in ourselves a glorious and expanding truth that cannot be stifled.

I did not stay in my church.

And I never joined another.

My Pentecostal family taught that truth did not originate in the authority of a church, nor in our limited ability to interpret the Bible, nor in another person. They taught *spirit witness*—that truth was evident in the soul, that we would know truth because our soul would feel it through the Holy Spirit, the only way to perceive God. In some ways, they gave me the tools to survive them because I know in my heart of hearts, in every cell breathing in my body and every electron dancing through my form, that I am exactly as this universe made me, as this universe wants me to be—and no interpretations, preachers, or churches can stand against this truth.

But communion is about more than truth.

It's a holy coming together, an intimate exchange of love.

I never joined another church, but I tried for the sake of communion. My husband and I live a five-minute walk from an affirming Episcopal church. I did my best to be a part of it. But I simply could not sit through a service. I simply could not personally find a way to feel God using rituals that have been used to harm me. The rituals themselves were beautiful, and I am sure that they are comforting, affirming, and beautiful to others, even other queer folks, but I think that for me, the damage has been done.

So instead of attending service, I cooked for these people who welcomed me in. Food was the first communion I ever knew, the first intimate sharing of love I ever felt, from my vulnerable infant self being held to my mother's breast in mornings I don't remember to toddler me being sat on the trailer floor in front of morning cartoons with a bowl of soft biscuit that my mamaw had baked and broke apart for me, covered in sausage cream gravy she had stirred up for me. For over a year, I made breakfast at that Episcopal church. Before service, me and my husband made buttery grits, bacon, toast, and scrambled eggs for the dozen or so older church members who showed up for it. Then, while he and the others attended service and together partook of the Holy Eucharist from the same hands of the same priest, eating from the same bread and drinking from the same cup, I stayed behind. I did the dishes. I wiped the tables. I returned the pots and pans.

I didn't share the reciprocal experience that the others had, no matter how much a part of me wanted to, but I soon learned that my breakfast communion was enough to fill me. I loved preparing food every week. I loved watching folks come in from the cold and have hot food waiting for them. I loved seeing folks talk and feel seen and enjoy a meal together. And it was enough just to cook. They did not have to feed me just because I fed them—because I had already been fed so many times in my life. I have felt that hunger met. I had been given all the love I needed through food, food as love poured into me by people who wouldn't break bread with me now, yet even still that imperfect love from the past swole up and could give of itself when the time came.

Communion, it seems, doesn't have to happen in the same space and time.

Communion, it seems, is something altogether bigger.

My husband never met Flannery O'Connor's mother, though he and I have visited their homestead a few times in our nearly two decades of marriage. But I do not doubt his communion with her, no matter how unlikely Regina Cline might have been to accept it had she been given the chance. He, too, has loved people who are homophobic. He, too, has *been loved* by people who are homophobic. His holiness rises from this broken space like morning fog from the dark of night, and his love for people who, because of their churches, don't always love him back is an act of communion, of whispering light in that darkness and saying to someone, "You matter to my universe whether or not I matter to yours." And, like the stories from *Queer Communion* that take up space in my heart and have been witnessed by the part of my spirit knowing truth, such love born in difficult places permeates the edges of universes and leaves all who feel it warmed by its holy glow.

Home is

Raychel Kool

Abecedarian poem, after "What Home Is" by Ashley Hope Pérez

Home is

algae-green cow ponds and apple pickin with aunts in Mawmaw's backyard and it's

blackberry pickin with baby cousins on my hip and beagle barks that bounce off the hills. But home is also

changin from my binder to my bra in the gas station bathroom.

Home is

deer heads on the wall (I used to hide them in my Snapchats) and deer meat in the deep freeze downstairs

and what I'm mostly tryin to say is that my home is

enough.

Home is

feelin the most at peace in my trans body when I'm with the trees in the woods behind my house—redbuds and honeylocusts and cedars and persimmons—my church.

Home is

goldenrod swayin in the pasture

and

huntin for old glass bottles down the crick holler.

Home is bein

invited to a snappin turtle fry in my neighbor's basement and feelin so loved there even with that MAGA flag in his yard

it's

"Jesus water" (cistern water) free of chlorine that I take back to school in two big bottles.

Home is

Kentucky, and katydids in the nighttime.

Home is

lily-orange bouquets gathered from roadside ditches

meat from cows we raised ourselves

naps on Mawmaw's front porch swing

old trees swollen over barbed wire fences.

Home is

petunias in the flowerbed and peepers in the pond; Preacher Mike denouncin queers and layin his hands on my shoulders to pray for my safe return to school, all in the same Sunday

it's that my

queerness sometimes feels like my family's best-kept secret.

Home is

roastin marshmallows for Reese's Cups s'mores

sandpaper tongues and the sweet breath of cows, snappin garden green beans into a five-gallon bucket

the trailer post office where I sent my first girlfriend love letters in heart-stickered envelopes.

Home is

uncles who remind the little cousins to eat their taters, uncles who take me for fast rides on their quads, and uncles who throw "fag" around like it's a hacky sack.

Home is

vetch on the side of the road

and

woodsmoke hangin from my dad's flannel coat.

Home is

excitement—contained, don't let her know it's a big deal—the first time my momma calls my friend "she"

and

yearnin for a future where she might also call me "they."

Home is a

zero-stoplight town—though I wouldn't call it a town—that holds me with hands that are calloused but not callous, flawed but tender, learnin, reachin.

Part One

MATRIARCHS AND MAMAWS

Nothing Can Separate Us from the Love

Savannah Sipple

Granny died on a Saturday afternoon in September, one day after she'd been released from the nursing care facility she had been in and out of since she broke her hip the previous April. She was eighty-six years old. When Mom told me Granny died, I left the literary open mic I was about to emcee and went to the hospital where Mom and my aunt sat vigil over Granny's body before they took her away. None of this matters, except I almost came out to my grandmother a few weeks before she passed.

Coming out is a process, and mine was long. I spent years terrified I might be gay and then even more years figuring out how to hide it. The good Christian people of my eastern Kentucky hometown let it be known that homosexuality was the worst kind of sin. And though I'd only ever known Granny to be kind to everyone, her faith did not waver. She followed the King James version of the Bible. My brother, my mom, my oldest friends—of all the people I came out to or postponed coming out to, Granny was the one whose love I couldn't bear to lose.

I say I almost came out to her because I was too scared to go through with it. I visited her in the care home where she was staying for rehabilitation. I took her some cornbread—the first food she taught me to make. Her physical therapist had just gotten back from her honeymoon, and Granny was telling me all about it and the photos she'd seen.

"That was the prettiest wedding. She looked so nice. . . . But I'll tell you, she married a woman."

My heart started to race a little as I said, "Well, Granny, people do that. Women marry each other because they love each other."

All she replied with was, "I know. They looked so happy," but it was enough to make me almost tell her. I wanted to tell her, and the way she bragged and bragged about her physical therapist made me think she might be able to wrap her mind around her own granddaughter loving a woman.

Some of my earliest memories revolve around the gymnastics and dance class I participated in for a few years. Alongside several of the girls I'd end up being friends with through high school, I tumbled, cartwheeled, and danced to my heart's content. Except I wasn't like the other little girls. I wasn't little. I was a head taller than everyone else and considerably heavier. My mother dressed me in the same leotards and outfits the other girls wore. Looking back, I'm surprised the recital costumes came in a size that fit me. I also remember that several of the mothers could sew. To top it off, I wasn't graceful. As in, during one recital, I clown-rolled the curtains down. As in, I tore them down. My friends and I still laugh about that and the way I'd forget some of the dance moves and turn to my best friend. She also watched me, so we mimicked each other, neither of us knowing the right steps. Mom made up my face and hot-rolled my hair, which hung to my butt, and I complained about being hot. To this day, I hate long hair because it burns me up. I stood out. I knew it and I hated it, but I also hold those memories, those friends, close. How can both these things be true? I wanted to fit in with the other girls, and I also did not want to wear the outfits and makeup and hair teased to heaven. It became a pattern, the longing to fit in while also understanding I was just different.

Granny's body was failing her.

She had raised four children and worked as a subsistence farmer while also caring for her disabled husband, who was left mostly paralyzed by a car wreck when my mother was seven. She was farm-stock strong, never stopped moving or talking, but age and hard work had taken their toll. In the last eleven years of her life, she survived a mild heart attack, bladder cancer three times, horrible swelling of her legs due to congestive heart failure, and a broken hip. It was only in the last two to three years of her life that she stopped working in the garden, and she only stopped canning the last two. She loved her family and was the center of its universe. She also loved Jesus and went to church as often as she could, and when she couldn't she watched church services on television. She had more faith in her little finger than most have in their entire bodies—faith in God and in people.

If there was one person or place growing up where I felt I could just be, it was with Granny. When I was with her, I never felt like I was lacking. With other people, I wasn't feminine enough, thin enough, smart enough, quiet enough, cool enough. Sure, I knew she wanted certain things for me, like to marry a good man and have a reliable job. Still, with her, I felt like I was enough. She let me be, and she spoiled me rotten.

As a little kid, I'd stand at our front door and cry when she left our house. When I was in college, she cried every single time I left home to drive the three and a half hours back to campus. We were attached to each other.

Her mild heart attack happened a week or so after I graduated college, and it was at that point I decided to take on the role of caregiver. She had helped raise me. I was living at home and unsure of my future plans, so I eagerly stepped into this role, both to help her and to take some stress off my mother. It was easier, you see, to focus on that responsibility than to face some hard truths about myself.

❧

I don't really remember watching the movie *Pretty Woman*, but I do remember listening to the soundtrack over and over. I'd push play on my cassette player and write down Peter Cetera lyrics as fast as I could, push stop, rewind, and write some more. I left those lyrics on the desk of a girl I thought was so cool. I was too young to really understand what the lyrics meant or why I felt compelled to give them to the girl, but I was old enough to hurt a little when I realized she'd quietly stuck them in someone else's desk.

The same year I wrote those lyrics, I gave my heart to Jesus during a particularly impassioned altar call at the holiness church where I was raised.

❧

I grew up the way Granny wanted me to, and what I'm assuming she would say was the most important way: a devout Christian. Mom took us to church every week. I got saved when I was seven and rededicated my life to Christ when I was fifteen and working at the local church camp. For the next few years, I tried to drown myself in religious devotion. I did all the things I was supposed to: went to youth group, worked at the camp, prayed at school, included Bible verses in my signature, listened to Christian music, studied my Bible, babysat for my youth group leaders. On the outside and to those looking in, I had a place to belong, and I felt horrible. Not because I didn't believe but because I still wasn't enough.

There were all these moments, you see, when I would wonder to myself, "Does this mean I'm gay?" Looking back, I probably had a crush on the girl I gave the lyrics to, and the older basketball player whose skills I admired, and the girl from Bible camp who was artsy, and the girl from Bible camp who loved soccer, and the girl I became friends with near the end of high school, and the smart girl from my first creative writing class, and the girl . . . and the girl . . . and the girl. But I couldn't or wouldn't let myself really think I might be gay. I was already teased for being too fat, too sensitive, too much of a jock.

I could not endure one more thing.

It wasn't enough to have faith; as a woman I was expected to submit. I wasn't supposed to question men's authority. I was supposed to dress more feminine instead of the jeans, T-shirts, and sandals I wore all the time. I was supposed to wear makeup. Lose weight. Keep my mouth shut. Ignore secular music. Attend Bible college. Find a man, but good God don't do anything to tempt him. My independent, somewhat feminist self never could fully give in to the church's expectations of me. But Granny would say my faith was what made me enough.

While working on my master's degree, I stumbled upon the movie *My Summer of Love* and became obsessed with Emily Blunt. I knew that was a crush. I kept the DVD hidden where no one would find it. There's this thing, I think, with women who love women, especially when you're first coming out, where you're not sure if you want to be with the woman you're crushing on or if you simply want to *be* her. The basketball player, the artsy girl, the writer in my class—all those girls—did I want to *be* them or *be with* them? My inability to recognize my queerness, to accept my sexuality for so long, makes it harder for me to know. Maybe I wanted to be with Emily Blunt. Maybe I just wanted to be so free that I'd fall for the local girl.

A couple of things came to a head that shifted my relationship with my grandmother. I went from a teenager who was scared she might be gay to a young adult who was pretty sure she was gay but had decided she would never act on it. It wasn't a sin unless you acted on it, right?

The problem with knowing I was gay but not acting on it was that I was denying myself a key component of the human experience: romantic love. I took pride in saying I would never be the girl who pined after a boy or who called their partner when they were visiting with friends, but the reality was that I would never be that girl because I was denying myself the opportunity to know that kind of love. I was at the same time also denying my whole self and all the culture and community that comes with being queer. There's a lot of self-loathing that goes into denying yourself some of these basic things. I had also never felt like I fully belonged anywhere: I wasn't girly enough, athletic enough, religious enough, or thin enough, and looking back, I can see how not accepting my queerness left me still stuck on the cusp of something. Hiding made me miserable, and I filled my time with anything that kept me busy, particularly work and family. But my sadness deepened to the point where I knew something had to give, and I was afraid it would be me.

I made the decision to try to come out. I knew that I would have to leave my hometown to do so. I also knew this likely meant I wouldn't be able to care for my grandmother the way I had for the past nine years. It killed me to leave her, not because she wouldn't be cared for but because we were so attached to each other. I knew, though, I had to find a way to build a life for myself—whether that was out and proud or with the closet door cracked or whatever else. I knew the way I was living was not allowing me to thrive.

The writer at the workshop, the poet I knew only through email, the Shakespeare professor: Did I want to be with them? How could I pray them all away?

I moved to Lexington, Kentucky, a whole hour and a half away from home, mainly because a lot of my friends lived there or near there and because it was close enough that I could be there for Granny if she really needed me. I spent the next year in a small apartment trying to make sense of myself. It didn't help that my mother had gotten a weekend job in Lexington and often wanted to spend the weekend at my apartment. I read a lot that year, and I spent much of the fall and winter watching shows like *The L Word* and *Queer as Folk* to try to learn more about queer culture. I was mostly clueless, and I was still living my life to help my family. Mom stayed with me many weekends. I traveled home to help Granny. I spent a lot of time helping with my best friend's children. These aren't things that I regret, but they also served as a great escape and kept me from having to face myself.

All the busyness also kept me from having to face other people. I had no idea how I'd ever come out to my family, and I wasn't sure how to even tell my friends. One saving grace was the fact that I had managed to make a few friends who were queer—most of them men. When I came out to my closest group of writer friends, two gay men and a lesbian, their response was, "Duh, we've known this a long time," which was both a relief and a validation. At this point, I knew I was gay, but in the edges of my mind, I still thought perhaps I could stay closeted.

❧

I am pretty sure I asked myself, "Does this make me gay?" up to the point where my writing mentor looked at me and said, "You're gay, right? So, let's hear it in your poems." Did I want to be her?

❧

I couldn't stay closeted. My mother lived with me for a year and during the last month of that, my grandmother lived with us, too. She was past the point of living alone and was not happy about the loss of her independence, and she was convinced my mother would move into a one-bedroom apartment and leave her with me. But I needed to be alone. I needed to come out.

❧

The writer from outside the mountains who once drove me crazy with her fancy accent.

❧

I've known my best friend since we were three. Our mothers grew up down the holler from each other. Her kids call me Auntie. Her kids kept me busy, and I was scared to death that I'd lose them, that I'd lose her friendship. I'd like to tell you it was easy, that our sibling-like relationship meant she adjusted quickly, and it wasn't ever hard. I can say she's managed to not walk away. Her kids still call me Auntie. I can say she treats my wife with love.

❧

The girl on the foundation board, the feminist with dark hair and great tits.

❧

Granny died on a Saturday afternoon. After they took her body, but before we left the hospital, I sat in my mother's car and talked about what needed to be done. At the mention of her funeral, Mom asked me to give the eulogy.

I said to her, "I won't wear a dress."

"You don't have to, but don't tease up your hair."

My pompadour was the bargaining chip. It would be three more months before I'd come out to my mother.

⊰ ⊱

The poet who once played basketball.

⊰ ⊱

My best friend and I argued theology for a while, quoting Bible verses and sending scholarly articles back and forth to argue the origins and meanings of poorly translated words. For a long time, I thought being gay meant walking away from my faith. Would it be heretical to say my faith carried me down the path to coming out, that the belief in love is just that strong?

⊰ ⊱

The bank teller who wore ties. The writer who wore oxfords and button-up shirts. The athlete who came out after winning the World Cup. Sometimes I'm still not sure if I wanted to love them or be them.

⊰ ⊱

I stood at my grandmother's visitation in black jeans, a white top, and brown Chelsea boots. I brushed my hair down. The morning of her funeral, I had coffee on my great-aunt's porch, overlooking her farm in eastern Kentucky. I kept thinking about loss, about Granny, about all the ways in which I have never felt at home. Mom and I planned her service, and I fought my aunt about song choices because Granny sure as hell wouldn't have wanted "Wind Beneath my Wings" played as the funeral recessional. I went with "Lullaby" by The Chicks because I'd included it on a video montage I made for Granny's eightieth birthday, and she loved the chorus.

In her eulogy I talked about all the ways the family was rooted to Granny, how she was our landing spot, our home, and there were moments when I had to stop because I couldn't breathe. As much as it had hurt to leave home to come out, it hurt more that I'd left Granny, that I hadn't been able to share this one part of me with her. The one thing. And it felt like the biggest. After the eulogy, I listened to the hymns I'd chosen. I sat through the altar call. Later that evening, I drove back to Lexington, took two Xanax, and finally slept.

There are moments in our lives when we know we're confident in the person we are, in the things we know to be true about ourselves. My moment was at her visitation, where I didn't know how I'd move forward without her. How did I manage to keep going? Is it fate or faith that a month after Granny died I met the woman I would marry? What would my grandmother say about this granddaughter of hers who now has a wife, who now has a love whose arms open wide enough to call me home? I'd like to think she'd call that holy. I'd like to tell her I've finally become exactly who she raised me to be.

Devil Stompin' Shoes

JULIE RAE POWERS

Mamaw could never really do a whole lot. She had cataracts, diabetes, varicose veins, and breathing problems. Most of my time spent with her as a young'n was watching *Young and the Restless* or casting out the Devil. Though I was small, five or so, I knew both of these things were very serious undertakings where drama was front and center. Soap operas in the afternoon, Devil stompin' in the evening.

After dinner, with a full belly, Mamaw unwrapped her oxygen hose from the machine, it was mustard yellow and well worn, then tucked each tube behind her ears, settling the two prongs just inside her nostrils. She dabbed her watering eyes with a kleenex and a prayer cloth that she was almost never without. Leaning on one hip, reclining onto her arm in her wallowed-in brown recliner, she huskily asked the tiny tomboy standing in front of her to help her cast out the Devil with a little chuckle as the oxygen bubbled. Huh, I ain't seen him around, I thought. Why would anyone even invite him in? Wait, I don't even know if this guy really exists. Feeling an itch of confusion then skepticism on my brain. She pointed to a pair of worn-out teal green house slippers and directed me to put them on. I always thought of that color as hospital green. I guess I always thought of her as hospital green; these shoes, the green rubbing alcohol she used to clean her skin before receiving an insulin shot, and all the souvenirs she brought back from her many hospital stays. She was an incredibly petite woman, 4'10" on a good day, but her house shoes still swallowed me up. I shuffled over to her, gripping the insides of the house shoes with my tiny toes, wide-eyed, waiting for further direction. A bumpin' gospel song came on. I recognized it as one of Mamaw's favorite gospel groups and one of mine by proximity. She only ever listened to gospel. Gospel of all kinds, but this group was one of her favorites. I don't remember anything about them other than it was a Black male gospel group from some time between the 1970s and this moment in the mid-'90s. Recently, I asked my family if anyone knew the name of this group she often requested me to put on for her, and none of them could even remember the group existing, let alone the name. It makes me wonder if I imagined it. I like to think it's a special fact about her that is all mine. A morsel of a memory of our devout matriarch.

As the music played she told me to cast out the Devil. You gotta stomp him out! Stomp! Stomp! Stomp! Pound the floor *real* hard with them Devil stompin' shoes. So I did just that. I lifted one house shoe then the other, bringing my small feet down with all my might. I kept imagining the Devil sitting in his recliner in Hell just like Mamaw was sitting in hers but that he was really annoyed by all the noise coming from above, exclamation bubbles hovering above his head. The version of the Devil I imagined was large, red, and cartoonish, turning up his TV louder and louder to drown me out. Mamaw and I giggled as I stomped to the music while she clapped. I remained skeptical of the reality of the Devil from start to stomp, but what I did believe in was this time of closeness with my Mamaw, seeing her lips peel back across her dentures, experiencing her deep belly laugh, and witnessing a moment of her experiencing spiritual pleasure with her grandchild when I usually saw her in pain.

A fever got ahold of me that my mama couldn't bring down with lukewarm oatmeal baths, cold packs, or tylenol so she carried me over to Mamaw and Papaw's house late in the night. We headed straight for Mamaw's room. Mom lay me across the lifted king-size bed then wrapped me in quilts as I shivered. I heard whispers as my head lolled around, my eyes slowly batting open then closed. Sometimes I heard quick conversations as Mamaw sent Papaw or Dad or whatever fetching boy down the hall or into the kitchen to collect all her necessities. Mamaw would assure Mom that it would get taken care of. That I would get taken care of. That the Lord abandons nobody. My shivers continued as I tried to open my eyes and delirium grabbed hold of me. The room was dark, with flickering gold liquid light that came from the antique lamp on Mamaw's nightstand then bounced off of her dresser mirror to make the room warm and fluid like a womb. Mamaw closed the door so we could have privacy as she communed with God to ask him to relieve me of my pain. My mom never left the room. She couldn't leave her baby in this state but also, there was so much to be learned from her mother-in-law and her relationship with God.

Warm, thick oil slipped from the middle of my forehead toward the bedsheets in a fat tear but was smoothly caught by my mamaw's thumb as she guided the blessed castor oil horizontally across my forehead while her lips moved fast. They moved fast but I heard nothing but a few rugged whispers of the Lord's name paired with *please*, then her tongue took over half of the work and began moving faster than her lips had before. Her full palm covered my forehead, other hand on my arm, my mother's hands landing wherever there was space left. The room smelled of fire light, oil, Jergens lotion, and another time. I went from understanding snippets to realizing what I was hearing was nothing I could figure out, a roiling of the tongue. Mamaw and Mom must've laid hands on me in prayer for an hour or longer. Time dragged on as I ached then fell asleep. I woke up several hours later in the early morning to voices outside the door. I got the feeling that none of them had gone to bed at all that night. I unrolled myself from my swaddle and climbed down onto the handmade step stool wrapped in carpet Papaw had made for Mamaw so she could get into the bed then eased up to the cracked-open door, trying to snatch as many adult conversation snippets as I could, one of my favorite pastimes. Mom was drinking coffee at the table when I emerged from the dim den of Mamaw's bedroom. She lit up and rejoiced! The Lord worked his ways. Her baby was better. My child's brain struggled with the facts of the story. I did feel so much better after feeling I was going to die. All it took was some blessed oil and a person of Mamaw's faith. One of God's angels. How could I be better so suddenly? Mamaw had a gift that somehow I knew I would never have.

The way my dad tells it, he wouldn't be alive if not for his mother's devotion to the Lord and her passionate prayers for the Lord to keep him through all of his self-inflicted danger. He recounts many reckless nights driving belligerently drunk through the winding mountain roads of coal country, wondering how he didn't drive off a cliff or kill someone or himself. How could he flip so many trucks upside down into creek beds and simply walk away, walk home before the cops came with no harm nor injury? His mother's faith. Her loyalty for walking with the Lord was rewarded with the extension of her children's lives.

She was just a few floors above me in the ICU the day I was born, struggling with fluid in her lungs. They say she almost didn't make it. I don't know if they said it was because I was on the way that she stuck around or if that was what I told myself. Somehow, without adequate explanation, I have felt this event connected us divinely. How, though we were both traversing spiritual planes in opposite directions of one another, we existed together in that liminal space between her dying and me coming to life, entering the world. An ethereal capsule holding us. More than a visual scene, it exists as a feeling, and that feeling pervades everything I know and have crafted of our experience. Pure love. Unencumbered by judgment, persecution, or expectation. Simply present and supportive. Occasionally, I imagine her turning to the archangel that day with a look that gently says, *not yet*.

I got ten whole years with her and plenty of episodes of *Young and the Restless*, though I discovered that *Days of Our Lives* was my soap of choice. Their airtimes overlapped, so we would start one then flip to the other during the commercials. After school I would walk across the bridge to our trailer, throw my school stuff down, and walk across the wood planks laid across the thirty feet of mud to her house. Usually Mom was napping, so I would spend time before dinner with Mamaw. We practically lived with her near the end of her life. In the early hours of the morning, I awoke to my mom whispering and cooing to Mamaw. She struggled for breath. My mom carried a look I had never seen before but encouraged me to either get ready for school or go back to bed. My cousins and I went to school that day like normal, then shortly after the day started I received a call over the intercom during first period that I was being checked out. An unsettling feeling came over me. My fifth-grade teacher caught my pause. "Julie, honey, you were called for check out." She said it softly and with some love. Her and I had a fun relationship where she would play pranks on me by taking the candy I wasn't supposed to have out of my desk and hiding it in a cup on hers. When I would start to look for it then squirm when I realized it was gone, she would cackle and reveal she was the culprit. She would never give my candy back in front of the class, but after the day or week was over she would call me over as the class emptied out to give it back to me with a little wink each time. Her tenderness was always present, but the shift in her tone of voice scared me, like she knew what I knew. That something bad must have been happening. As I walked to the school office I ran into my two cousins in the hall, same look of unease on both of their faces, asking me if I knew what was going on. Surprisingly, none of our regular caretakers were waiting for us. Out in front of the school stood our fun older cousins who we all were obsessed with. More confusion.

At first there was silence in the car on the way home then some misdirecting with fun, light conversation. Finally, us younger cousins interrupted to ask what exactly was going on. Mamaw wasn't doing well. The family thought we should come home from school to be with her. More silence followed as we realized what this news likely entailed.

Mamaw was in her daybed in the living room like usual, but her face was a combination of colors I recognized only as a very bad sign. Her breathing was irregular, shallow, her ribs wracking. After I had gone to school, Mamaw died right in front of Mom, just the two of them. I overheard Mom telling the story as I held Mamaw's hand, feeling the gnaw of death in my chest. Mom immediately began resuscitating her, screaming, *Don't leave me like this, not like this, not alone like this. You come back. You can't do this to me, Midge.* Imagining my mom pumping her chest with grief-filled desperation flooded my ten-year-old spirit with terror. After she was revived, Mom began making phone calls for the family to join her and possibly say their last goodbyes.

The adults sent all of us kids out to the tire swing as Mamaw's condition worsened. Several of us kids protested about being ushered out of the house, knowing what was about to happen. It was mostly the younger kids outside kicking around rocks unenthusiastically, pacing, trying to decide what exactly would happen to Mamaw once she decided to leave us. An older cousin came out of the house looking distraught, which caused me to bolt toward the porch and into the house. As I stormed through the side door, through the kitchen, one of my eldest boy cousins with his strong biblical name caught the torpedo of my body, saying, *She's going, she's gone, let her go.* My body was still running, my mind still propelling me forward though I was caught in his strong arms, as I caught sight of her very last breath over his shoulder, realizing I was entirely too late. Mamaw had a way of making you feel like her spirituality, her love of the Lord and from the Lord, extended out to you, that you were divine all on your own. Worthy by virtue of *simply being* a child of God. Her passing broke my ten-year-old heart in a way that I have not felt since, but I took away that feeling of being vibrantly loved and worthy. The messaging I heard throughout my life from other Christians and broader society in regard to being queer eroded away that sense of being loved and worthy. It seemed as if my queerness exempted me from spirituality in its entirety. I have wondered if she had been around, what my experience as a queer person from Appalachia might have been like. Would I have still felt divine, worthy, and loved in her presence? Would I receive judgment and a lashing? Would she have been my biggest advocate? Would she have protected me?

I navigated my life without that feeling for a long time until I found queer community. Longtime friends connected to their witchiness cast spells for my safety, my partner mixes herbs and trinkets for financial abundance, my housemate rubs my back as I scream with grief in the yard. All feelings and states worthy and valid by nature of existing under our brilliant sun, together. In a world of fascist ideologies, I have learned that queerness is spiritual in its own right. That simply coming into being and surviving in this world is an act of spiritually defiant, radical soul resilience.

The Faith of My Mothers

Matthew Jacobson

My Catholicism is everything to me. It's my baptism that has given me a living and heavenly awareness that I am never alone in my communion of saints and sinners. It is my lens through which I see that all of creation is Good and my destiny is intrinsically connected to the health of this universe, our earthly home. It is the love language that I seek and find God in all things, especially my marriage. It is the whisper of peaceful presence on dark nights and the glorious triumph of each new day. It is radical news from Rome on social justice issues of war, care for the ecology, and human trafficking. It is unconditional love and embrace for the immigrant, transperson, and prisoner. It is the measure of my relational efforts with my human sisters and brothers that demands I constantly ask myself "When, Lord? When did I see you hungry, alone, or sick?" I love stained glass windows, the smell of incense, and little statues of curious historical figures who have also walked this earth over the past couple millennia. I believe ritual and retreat can transform the hearts and minds of all people. I believe in resurrection and that death is not the last word. I feel the fire of mission within me when I hear the call of the birds, the chants of the protesters, the cries of the poor, the harmony of singing in one song. I believe in the communion of all things and hope that one day all humankind will rise up and be one family like Jesus hoped for when he prayed "that they may be one, as you and I are one." And I believe that God, Heaven, and all our relations are right here with us, journeying along with our struggles and hopes, cheering us on and loving us through this unnecessarily challenging world.

I left West Virginia when I was nine years old under scary circumstances of abuse, housing instability, and financial insecurity. My parents' divorce was dangerous and traumatic. I became my mother's caregiver in her codependent immaturity. I've spent the rest of my life seemingly trying to overcome those things and piece together the pieces of who I am into an integrated person. Yet, deep within me, I'm still that awkward fat kid keeping my shoulders high and my head low, waiting for the next shoe to drop. I'm still afraid of doing without—without food, money, friends, safety, and on and on. I want to take that kid by the hand and walk him through the next forty years and tell him, *You are a beloved child of God and God will be your parent when your parents can't fulfill their role. Love is on your side and always will be. Sometimes you have to leave the place you're from to find the world is your Home. Your ancestors are with you cheering you on, always. You have a purpose, and the seeds of God's hope are planted within you. Do not be afraid; you are going to see many wonderful things.*

Like being an Appalachian from West Virginia, I can never disassociate myself from the roots of my spiritual being because of a long line of powerful and spiritual women. Women like my great-grandmother Maria Nachmann Boyer, who immigrated to this country with her brother from Slovakia. She had in her pocket her blue-gemmed rosary and some family recipes. I still feed off those sacred elements she brought over. From her came my grandmother, Mama Kees. Maxine Frances Boyer Kees Moore was an elegant career woman and also had a lethal double-edged tongue. She was the definition of a mountain mama and survivor. She grew the most beautiful gardens, took care of the roses in Ritter Park, and worked at the town newspaper and then the VA hospital; she was the first woman president of the American Legion Post 16, and she gave birth to four kids with terminal illnesses. She had an impenetrable determination to endure through hard times and never stopped worrying about how her children could survive their kidney disease and live for as long as possible. She also hated the fact I was gay. She was convinced I was going to either die of AIDS or be killed because of it. That is, until I introduced her to the man I would marry; then everything changed. To her, he was "My Brian," and she showed him the secrets of making a perfect baked potato and the joy of having a beer in the garden. She loved showing off her garden overflowing with roses, blueberries, daisies, blackberries, tiger and calla lilies, and black-eyed Susans, tons of black-eyed Susans. She loved him with all her heart . . . and made me sleep on the couch, you know, because we weren't married.

My mother, Monica Frances Kees Jacobson, was a deeply spiritual woman. And if you ask anyone who knew her, they will tell you she was hilarious. She could defuse any situation with silly faces, painfully great puns, and funny voices. She was very good at masking her pain and low self-esteem with humor. She was seemingly simple and meek, but I knew the woman was profound in her own way. She never gave up her belief that no matter how hard life was, God would provide. God was an abiding presence who knew our prayers, our struggles, our fears. My mom died twenty years ago now, in 2004, and it wasn't pretty. It was the hardest of times as she declined in her physically deconditioned and drug-addicted prison of depression. We fought all the time. She had the short-lived selflessness to let me go and forge my own path. And perhaps I was growing too far away and it hurt her immensely. I wanted out. Out of WVa, out of her house, out of her life, and as far away as possible. I knew it was the drugs, the quart-size bottles of Oxy-this and Percocet-that, that had killed my mother's instincts to survive. She had survived a broken childhood and an abusive marriage. She lost all of her friendships, her church, her family, her identity, and the support of her government, which she gave her life to during Vietnam. She had become a statistic of the opioid massacre that stole the soul of my hometown and our wild, wonderful state. I had a dream soon after she died. She was in some sort of eternal care unit of a hospital and as I pulled back the curtain to her room, she was being cared for by a couple of "angel-nurses" who were helping her get adjusted to a new gown. She looked at me and said, "I'm not sick anymore. I love you, Matthew, just give me some time and I'll be better again." Did she come to me from a heavenly rehab of some sort? Did my spirit need to imagine her in a place of healing? I'm not sure, but even in her death, I believe she and I can both experience the healing power of forgiveness, restoration, and love. My Catholicism gives me the freedom to believe that death is not the end—in fact, there is no end with everlasting love.

I know personally these systems of church, government, and health care are not perfect and can harm people as much as they are created to help them. We were all born into these institutions of dysfunction, and the Catholic Church is too many times the star of that show. But my mom taught me that the power of love through actions can break through systems of injustice. We moved to Dayton, Ohio, from Huntington, West Virgina, when I was in third grade to escape the terror of my father's abuse and so my mom could find better work. There, we became members of Corpus Christi parish and school. Our priest was beloved by the community. He was a tall, strapping man who wore leather and rode a motorcycle. He lived alone across the parking lot from school. A beautiful house just for one man. He must've been lonely. He became ill. They said it was a kind of tuberculosis and it could be cured with orange juice. We would have orange juice fundraisers for our parish priest when he was hospitalized. Because of her nursing background, my mom recognized his physical ailments and viral symptoms. She knew that orange juice wasn't going to cure what he had. While he was still active in his duties as our parish priest, I would walk to school early in the morning while my mom was working the overnight shift so I could serve at Mass before school. One time, before Mass had begun, he criticized my mom for not making tuition payments on time. I told him she was working at that very hour and doing the best she could. He shamed me in front of my classmates. As they put on their garments of liturgical service, he said I could not serve at the altar again until my mom paid up on tuition. I remembered the story of the Good Shepherd and was mad and embarrassed. Here was our shepherd putting us out into the darkness and cutting us off from the community. *Whoever will not receive you or listen to your words—go outside that house or town and shake the dust from your feet* (Matthew 10:14).

That priest was eventually removed from our parish because of his illness and decline. He disappeared and died, and no one talked about it. Soon after he died, my mom was working the overnight shift. I was getting ready to leave for school when I saw her sitting on the couch in her nursing uniform. She told me she had just been fired for holding a dying man who had AIDS. She knew he was gay, and no family or friends came to see him. She saw the other nurse slide his tray of food across the floor as the man lay dying in his bed in his own filth. She cleaned him up, changed his sheets, fed him his meal, and held him as he cried on her shoulder. He was afraid of dying alone. When the nurse manager saw the man resting his head on my mom's shoulder, they fired my mom for being exposed to his viral tears. She was so mad at the staff, and although we struggled to keep the electricity on ourselves, her only worry was for that man dying alone in his quarantined and abandoned ward of the nursing home. As I walked to school, I was proud of my mom and knew she had done something right and just. And then I remembered we already struggled with money, and I was scared. And then I began thinking about those who looked down on us for being poor, weird, hillbillies . . . and I remembered the feeling of shame from our priest. I was thinking about these things as I walked past the rectory and wondered "was anyone there to hold Father as he was dying?" My mom taught me the Catholic values of compassion and resisting systemic evils by being an instrument of incarnate love. She showed me that love reaches through fear and embraces. She taught me to seek out the isolated and lonely and love them as if they were Christ himself. Now I hold people as they are dying and I pray they know nothing but love as they take their leave from this broken world, because that's how my mom taught me.

When our poverty hit its darkest days, I was in seventh grade. We were living days and weeks without a phone and electricity because there wasn't enough money to keep those things on. I was walking to the food pantry for food and getting the rest of our groceries with whatever food stamps we had. My mom was getting late with the rent and the new landlord had just sent a note to her saying we were going to be evicted if she didn't pay up. My mom sat me down and explained that she couldn't afford the Catholic high school and that I would likely have to go to the neighborhood public school. I was terrified of that school. The police were always there, and I saw those kids lighting the dumpsters on fire and terrorizing the neighborhood. I had grown up in an educational system that was always demanding we lived in service of God and the world. That sense of mission-driven learning was my safety net and source of hope for our future. And then, one day after school when the phone and electricity happened to be on, I got a phone call. It was my principal, Sister Judith Gutzweiler. She wanted to speak to my mom and told me to have her call when she got home from work. Needless to say, although I had spent many days in detention, I could not think what I had done wrong that day. So, I cleaned the whole house top to bottom, including washing the porch—penance for a sin I wasn't sure I committed, but question marks are no match for Catholic guilt!

When my mom came home to see my penance, she looked at me sternly and asked, "What did you do?!" I said I didn't know, but Sister wanted her to call her back. When my mom rang her up, Sister wanted to meet my mom the next morning before school to talk to her. When my mom asked what I had done wrong, Sister laughed and said, "Nothing this time, but I'm hoping what we have to talk about may be an answer to your prayers." I remember watching my mom leave the school building the next morning, just as the bell was ringing at the start of the day. She had a distant look on her face, but she didn't look mad. Moments later I was called to the principal's office. *Mea culpa . . . again.*

Sister Judith began asking me how things were at home, and I told her about our poverty and financial struggles. She asked what I wanted to be when I grew up and if my mom and I had talked about high school or college. I told her about being an astronaut or a doctor. I also told her about us considering the local public high school and my fears of that. She then produced a pamphlet about a residential scholarship program for boys in Cincinnati called Boys Hope. If I applied and was accepted, they would pay for me to go to high school and then get a scholarship to college. It was a Jesuit Catholic program, and I would likely go to the all-male Jesuit college prep high school called St. Xavier. Jesuit Catholic priests believe in this life-changing philosophy called *cura personalis*, which means "care for the whole person." This Jesuit program believed that if a child is cared for mind, body, and soul, then they will thrive academically, socially, and ultimately professionally, releasing them from the cycle of poverty. I was terrified. All boys? College prep? Move away from my mom and live in a group home? I was energized with the kind of terror and intrigue where you know that whatever you decide, your life will never be the same. Little did I know, at age twelve, what Sister Judith was opening up for me was the path for my future, a path that indeed was a gift from God and could provide us the only possibility I could have to escape poverty. *"For surely I know the plans I have for you," says the Lord. "Plans for good and not for harm, to give you a future, a hope"* (Jeremiah 29:11).

My mom and I talked about what this would require of me: moving to Cincinnati, leaving her at home sick and alone, getting a world-class education, and having the chance to live the life God intended for me. My mom recalled that when I was born, we both coded. I had been choking on my umbilical cord, which was wrapped around my throat three times, and clutched onto her uterus and pulled it out with me. The doctors had to punch her womb back into her, revive me, and stop her bleeding. We both received Last Rites and an emergency Anointing, and I was baptized in the operating room. After the chaos subsided and we were both stable, my mom said, she held me knowing that both of us were now living miracles. She told me she said a prayer of thanks to God and said, "He's yours now, God, take care of him." She said she believed Sister Judith's invitation was God's response to her prayer back in that army hospital. *The Lord hears the cry of the poor* (Psalm 34).

During my interview process I would finally meet the woman who would change everything in my life. With the greatest Cincinnati-Irish humor, structure, discipline, and faith, Sister Cookie Crowley sat across from me and explained the expectations of the program to me: always do my best, get involved in extracurriculars, get a job, and keep up with the academic rigors of being in a college prep program. She was wearing blue jeans, white tennis shoes, a Kelly green softball windbreaker that said "Crowley's," and buttons that said "Kiss me I'm Irish." She asked if I had any questions. I asked if she was really a nun. She leaned into the table and said, "You bet your ass I'm a nun."

Sister Cookie took the reins of reordering my dysfunctional past into a hopeful future. I was grounded all the time and had a bad attitude, and because of the adolescent chip I had on my shoulder, she and I butted heads often. But she was working me out with tough love and molding me into an independent, self-confident, and caring person. She demanded that I simply be a kid for the first time in my life. I didn't need to worry about food insecurity anymore (she was an EXCELLENT cook). I didn't have to be afraid of being evicted anymore. I didn't have to save my mom. I was in a safe neighborhood for the first time, and I loved my school. Sister Cookie taught me to find and serve God in all people and things, live by the rules of laughter and compassion, and be steadfast in my efforts for social justice. She also drilled into me that although I should never forget where I came from, I should also never forget that God gave me a new direction—so I should not be afraid to leave the nest and find my place in the world. The Catholic Church has never recognized the efforts of our religious women and their capacity for leadership since the days when Mary Magdalene was the first witness of the Resurrection. But it is precisely due to the vocational commitment of women like the Sisters of Charity in Cincinnati that I exist at all. I tremble at the thought of what would've happened to me if Sisters Judith and Cookie hadn't invited me to consider my future by leaving everything and everyone I had ever known behind and taking a leap of faith. *Take up your cross and follow me . . . for whoever loses his life for my sake will find it* (Matthew 16:24–25).

How far is Heaven? I currently live an hour east of the "Almost Heaven, West Virginia" state line, so I firmly believe Heaven's not that far *for those who have eyes to see and ears to hear.* I call upon Heaven all the time, and not just because I'm a hospital chaplain and it's my job. Rather, I believe the roots of faith have been planted in me like seeds in the garden of my family story. I believe that the Creator of all things has given me the chance of a lifetime to pass on the courage of my foremothers to my children. I believe I can call upon their spiritual help and heavenly parenting anytime. Stargazing is my favorite form of prayer. In fact, on a select few nights during intense prayer, I will look up to witness three shooting stars in a row: my trinity of mountain matriarchs giving me a sign they are still with me. Other nights I will follow the constellations and recall their stories. I can't help but lift my prayers up to the heavens for help, for company, for solace, for celebration, for lament . . . for everything.

I want to share with you, the reader, the story of how we came to be parents. I was working as the palliative care chaplain at WVU Medicine in Morgantown. After living my life running from WVa, I had finally found myself at home working with fellow mountaineers, ensuring comfort in times of great pain and grief. I loved it. But my husband was getting recruited back to Chicago, and we were going to have a conversation over Thanksgiving on whether we were going to stay in WVa or move back to Chicago. Everything I had prayed for on my journey to become a professional hospital chaplain had come true. Everything except kids. I always knew I wanted my kids to be from WVa. One starry and cold night alongside the Mon River, I built a fire and prayed to my heavenly mothers, including Jesus's mom, Mary. I prayed to St. Francis of Assisi too. I feel I have him to thank for my vocations as husband, father, and chaplain. As I finished my prayer, which went like, "Hail Mary full of grace, we need some kids in this place," I toasted the sky and finished my bourbon glass, hoping my prayers went somewhere close to God's hopes for Brian and me. And it happened again—three shooting stars falling right over our home, lit up by the river. All I could do was muster the word "amen."

The next morning, I got a phone call at work from the state of West Virginia about "two little stinkin' cute girls" who needed a foster family who would be willing to consider them for eventual adoption. I hung up the phone and turned my prayer back upward, saying, "Hail Mary, what I meant to say was '*child*,' SINGULAR, preferably under the age of two. But, thy will be done!" And then I drove down I-79 through the rolling hills to pick up our children and bring them to their forever family. Six months later, we decided to move back to Chicago, once again leaving the place I call Home to give our kids a better chance in the world. Three years later, after we had moved back to our community in Chicago, we would get another call from the state about their new sibling brother. Our family was continuing to unfold in our becoming whole with three stellar kids. I was scared poopless to be a parent. That is, until I came to remember I have been equipped by some of the most daring, bold, loving, and fearless women on earth. Women who sacrificed their very lives for the next generation. Women who weren't afraid of leaving a familiar home for the dream of the next generation. Women who sowed the seeds of resilience, wisdom, charity, and endless love in the earth of my soul. Because of them, I am. And because of God's love through them, our family will continue to grow through the hard times with laughter, tears, and lots of good food.

I thank God for the women in my life. Because of them I live life abundantly and take the greatest pleasure in serving others. My great-grandmother Maria wanted to grow a new life and taught me that leaving home is sometimes the only option available and not to be afraid when God is your companion. My grandmother Maxine shared my love of learning, food, and gardening. She also showed me the joy of loving my husband and gave me the gift of her ultimate acceptance. She deeply feared for my life as a gay man, until she finally met her "My Brian" and, after realizing being gay was simply our way of loving and being loved, he became her favorite everything. Although my mom's death was unfortunately very painful and left many open wounds, she taught me as a parent we should do everything for our kids, even give them to God when it's time to let them go. And when it comes to living my life in joyful authenticity, I cannot be more grateful for Sisters Judith and Cookie. When I came out as gay to Sister Cookie she said, "Tell me something I don't know!" She followed that with, "I hope you know I will always have your back. I love and support you no matter what." She was the voice of God's unconditional and everlasting love and acceptance. She also calls my husband her "My sweet Brian." I love how she has embraced Brian with the openness and joy that only a mother can.

The image of a garden and the seeds of faith resonates with my family story. No matter how ill-fated our story was and was to be, there was always a garden. My great-grandmother always had a lush garden of tomatoes, cabbage, roses, irises, and more. A few years ago, I drove past her empty house at 135 Sycamore Street, and I saw those irises growing along the side of the house. I remember planting them with her in first grade. So I jumped out, wandered around the empty shell that used to house our faith and family story, and dug up some of those irises with a broken coffee cup I found behind her old garage. Was it her cup? Did she pray over this cup of broken jadeite glass? I'll never know. But I got enough of those irises to transplant a bunch back with me, and they are still blooming in Chicago. Everywhere we have ever lived, we've left a garden. It is a legacy I continue with my own kids. I think it simply stems from our family's value of *leave the world a better and more beautiful place than when we got there.*

My WVa family is practically all gone now; they've all died away, mostly from the illness known as polycystic kidney disease. But I know my grandmother died a young death from the grief and energy it took to care for the disease. Folks will never know the grief she carried watching her children die long, slow deaths from the moment they were born into this world. I don't know if anyone else knows how my immigrant great-grandmother settled in WVa. She was from a family of Slavic glassblowers, and we had a special golden recipe for cranberry glass that the streams of WVa minerals could illuminate as brilliant. I don't know how many people know how she worked with the bishop to form a new parish on the outskirts of town where the working class and poor were because they needed Jesus out there and couldn't get to the city to attend the central Catholic Church. I don't know how many people know my uncle was the first person baptized in our parish, and that meant the world to my great-grandmother. I don't know how many people know my grandmother's baby grand piano sits at the front of that church, the same piano I played on as a toddler and hid inside of with my Star Wars figures. Yes, our family illness stole their futures, and the insanity of poor health care coupled with overmedicating veterans drove many of them down an addicted spiral of mental illness. They were so dysfunctional, so broken. And I'd give anything to see or hear them again. But my Faith assures me that the Kingdom is at hand, Heaven isn't some far-off place, they are near, and I believe they hear our prayers.

And so, each holiday I make a dish from their recipe cards. I'll set the table with the same Irish hospitality and lilt that Sister Cookie taught me. For my children, who will never meet their loved ones on my side, I tell and retell their stories to pass on our family and faith's values of hospitality and community. I tell them about our immanent and loving God. I tell them how to be discerning and listen for God in our hearts, how to build relationships everywhere we go, to be kind and grow love, to seek out the lost and forgotten. I tell them how to lay down our life for Christ means to be so compassionate to our neighbor that we may lose our job for it. And finally, that when God's love comes to us in the form of a spouse or child, we are called to simply say YES to God's gift and desire for us to love and be loved. And to say that I get to live this life with the man I love is the glue that holds this journey all together. I love how Brian loved my family through all their faults. And I love how every one of them loved him as their own.

I can never see myself, or any other human, as outside the Body of Christ. *The world is charged with the grandeur of God*, and we are all beloved. When we go forth to love and serve the Lord, we all have the ability to change the world for the better, or at least leave it better than we found it. It was because strong, faithful, hilarious, and hospitable women recognized my potential that I am who I am. I promise to live my life as a song of thanks for them and for the chance to live my one precious and wonderful life to the fullest. I will remember the hard times so I can appreciate the good ones. I will celebrate because suffering is fleeting and joy is eternal. I believe that love is the most powerful force in the universe, can heal all wounds, and brings all of us into communion with each other. I vow to pass those stories and seeds of survival on to our children as we remember, we celebrate, and we believe for another generation. May the Force be with all of us . . .

Ad Maiorem Dei Gloriam.

Emogene's Rosary

Emma Cieslik

I was born six years after my Grandma Emogene passed from breast cancer. From the day I was born, my parents asserted that I was not named after her. Many an aunt and uncle disagreed, however, seeing me as a tribute to their mother who died because a doctor failed to check for a cancer recurrence. My parents never wanted to name me or my sister after anyone, believing it set an expectation we had to live up to. My aunt and uncle were not alone. At a family reunion years later, Emogene's sister Jane—then struggling with dementia—fully believed that I was Emogene visiting her again in the flesh.

My relatives tried correcting great-aunt Jane, but it was no use. I was a dead ringer for her sister with her wide black eyes, a round face, and dimpled smile.

Emogene lived in Louisville, Kentucky, where she and my Grandpa Stanley raised my uncle—a Catholic priest—my aunt, and my dad. My Grandma Emogene and Grandpa Stanley were longtime parishioners of St. Barnabas on Hikes Lane. My mom's parents—Nonnie and Papa Joe—attended St. Martha's Catholic Church on Klondike. Both of my parents studied at parochial schools and were among many families affiliated by parish rather than neighborhood. I was baptized by my uncle, who claimed dibs on all my Sacraments at birth.

Thus I was born in Louisville to a devout Catholic family, all of whom lived in my old Kentucky home. So when my dad's work gave him an ultimatum during an early 2000s economic recession—a severance package or moving to the Chicagoland area—it wasn't much of a choice. But it was a "decision" that both families saw as a betrayal, choosing to leave hundreds of cousins, aunts, and great-uncles to raise their two daughters—my sister and me—in the big city. In truth, we grew up in a suburb a stone's throw from the Wisconsin border, surrounded by corn, soybean, and wheat fields.

To mend the divide, my sister and I split our childhoods between Louisville and Crystal Lake, driving home six or seven times every year. We had at least three Christmases, one usually spent at my uncle's museum of a house filled with JFK and Lincoln memorabilia. My Louisville family returned the favor only two times—my father's family drove up north only for my First Communion and Confirmation. Thus religion was cemented as the backbone of both families, whether praying over plastic tablecloths in Nonnie's kitchen or chatting with my uncle's priest friends at New Year's.

In all honesty, as a kid with undiagnosed OCD, my childhood is mostly radio static—sometimes a hazy image appears, but most of the time there's nothing. It's the same for my dad; however, my mom and sister remember being babies. My last memory of Louisville is a sad one: returning in 2015 to bury my last grandparent, Nonnie. Up until this past Easter, when I returned to Louisville with my family, I refused to go home. I felt it was retribution for all the hurt my extended family inflicted on my parents, who were blamed for our distance.

They couldn't have me, I thought. I wouldn't give them the satisfaction.

But last month I gathered with my mom's family on Bardstown Lane. I savored what few memories I had of this place: Papa Joe convincing my sister and me that his landlocked Kentucky backyard was once covered by ocean by planting seashells along his fence. Nonnie nibbling on a piece of fried cod from Hungry Pelican all night long, refusing to take the whole thing. Chasing down Grandpa Stanley's cat and drinking purple Kool-Aid from those wax bottles. Running past Nonnie and Papa Joe's bushes, rumored to be where the boogieman lived.

It was no coincidence that the first time I returned home in five years was for the holiest day of the year for Catholics. It was the day that women were the first to testify to Christ's resurrection. So on the day of celebration, I sang a prayer of reconciliation.

Growing up in a largely Polish, Irish, and Italian Chicago suburb, it never occurred to me that Catholicism was not the mainstream religion nor that any other religion existed until I entered middle school. I spotted many of my classmates at St. Thomas the Apostle every Sunday; one of my friends is even studying to become a priest. My mom taught my religious education classes, moving year to year with me, until I was confirmed. The Arby's and McDonald's down the street even advertised openly for Lent.

I wasn't involved in the church youth group, deeming the St. Thomas's gang too performatively pious. Instead, I attended one retreat in middle school that pulled a page right out of the evangelical Christian playbook. At the retreat, we were led in prayer for our future husbands to find us, received Mary Kay makeovers despite being told to foster beauty within ourselves through purity of mind and body, and, in a not-so-covert ceremony, walked a white rose up the central aisle of the after-hours church to place in a vase on the altar beside a statue of Mary bedecked in her purity colors.

This was especially harmful for a kid with undiagnosed OCD who was told by her CCD program head that thinking about a sin was just as bad as committing it. Venial or mortal, having the thought itself necessitated reconciliation. To a queer kid, this made every parish-mandated confession a game of choosing which sins to substitute for the real thing.

My dad's parents both had Catholic funerals, overseen by the Rattermans' Funeral Home, owned by a close friend of my uncle. The Rattermans even loaned my parents a black limo for their wedding. And my most prized possession is my Grandma Emogene's rosary.

Emogene was diagnosed with cancer right after she had my dad, and it took and took from her, first her hair then her strength. She kept fighting, wearing the paint off her rosary beads from so much prayer. Today, the beads are clear and grooved into the shape of Emogene's fingers—Hail Marys held in its chains.

I loved that rosary growing up because I believed that it had power within it. Raised Catholic, I was surrounded by objects I knew contained holiness, from prayer card relics to bottles of water from Lourdes to a small statue of Mary I kept long after both of her hands were knocked off. To me, it made complete sense—that some objects could contain a sacred power within them. As a kid growing up, I dreamt that one day, that power could live inside of me.

But I was taught from a young age that the best thing I could aspire to be one day was a saint. I wasn't convinced—the video my parish's CCD director showed us when I was growing up explained that the first step to becoming a saint was to die, often in deeply upsetting ways. While saints are beatified based on miracles performed after their death, they didn't officiate these miracles. Instead, they served as intercessors on our behalf to God, or to people in Heaven who were able to put a bug in God's ear.

In truth, I didn't want to be a saint.

According to this video, I wasn't even qualified, and many were classified based on their type of martyrdom. No, weird little Emma wanted to be an angel. I wanted the liberatory power of a being who didn't have to answer to human constructs like gender and sexuality. Angels could be anyone, I was told—that person in the Wendy's dining room or that little old lady at Joann's. They hid in plain sight and could shape-shift, wielding divine powers that they used for good. It felt predestined—the nurse had even mistaken me for a boy when I was being born.

But I was specific. I didn't want to be the hypermasculine angels my childhood priest Fr. Jerome described. In one of his homilies where he worked off crumpled coffee napkin notes, he said that we exist in a state of spiritual warfare. He didn't want those cutesy dutesy cherubs, he argued, he wanted an angel carrying a semiautomatic, white robes changed out for camo print and bandoliers crossing his chest. It was a John Rambo type of angel that also coincided with a growing conservative push at St. Thomas. This included political proselytizing from the pulpit, much to my mom's dismay.

You see, I saw Emogene as my guardian angel. It felt fitting. I was unofficially named after her and bore her face. While we never met, I felt a close personal connection with her growing up. She was my spiritual warrior. I believed she was a stand-in for Mary herself, who looked down on me and provided guidance amid the chaos of a queer Catholic childhood. Instead of a nondescript guardian angel, Our Madonna of Emogene facepalmed year after year as I broke my wrist three times because of my gangly legs. And while she was no Terminator angel, I believed Emogene was much more ferocious.

Growing up with an intense fear of the dark, I wielded Emogene's rosary like a spiritual mace. Night after night I couldn't fall asleep, and so I would whip out her rosary and pray so intensely it annoyed my sister. I liked to cluck my tongue, inflecting an unheard word in each prayer. I genuinely believed that perfect pronunciation of an unsaid prayer made it even more powerful. I lost Emogene's rosary behind my bed many, many times, but I saw it as my St. Benedict's medal and font of holy water—a tool to exorcize the demons hiding in the corners of my bedroom, laundry room, and mind.

See, my Grandma Emogene was so good at fighting cancer that doctors brought her in just to motivate patients who had given up. She personified cancer, just as the Church does the Devil, and instructed everyone she met to fight the disease like it was a real person. For her, cancer was a bodily war, just as keeping hope was a spiritual one. Like me when I was afraid of the dark or was struggling with then undiagnosed celiac disease or recurring sinus infections, she turned to her trusty Hail Marys. Glory Bes and Our Fathers were okay, but Hail Marys always came through.

I was an angry kid, and likely because of this I pictured Mary and my Grandma Emogene as the embodiment of female rage. I personally held a vendetta against Robert Bosch, my father's company's long dead founder, for forcing us to move. At their annual family picnics, I even went around asking for Robert. To me, Emogene crushed cancer beneath her feet the same way Mary stomped on Satan himself in Genesis. Even though Emogene lost her battle with cancer, I have no doubt that she turned around at the Pearly Gates just to spit in its face. I felt the same way about the church.

Even as a kid, I had my misgivings. When I asked my mom why the catechism said that gay people couldn't get married, she said that was just the way things were. Well, that wasn't good enough for little old Emma. She had her stubborns up. First she couldn't get married to a woman, next she was told to pray for a husband she didn't want, then she was told to remain chaste of mind—nearly impossible for a queer kid walking through Victoria's Secret with her mom. She was told to confess her sins but not the queer ones, to be truthful without being blatant, to stop sinning while still being herself.

She couldn't be an angel, despite all of the mourners at her grandparents' funerals claiming that Heaven got another angel! All of this made little baby Emma livid. What was she supposed to do? How was any woman, much less any queer woman, supposed to exist in the church? Many times as a child I thought about leaving the church, going to Mass and letting my mind drift elsewhere while the priest chattered on about Suzy Creamcheese and Billy Box O'Donuts—I kid you not, these are the real names that he used. But she worried about the consequences, about giving up her spiritual protector.

As someone who struggled with chronic illness, I was often overwhelmed by pain, fatigue, and stress. In those moments, I always turned to Emogene for help and pulled out that same rosary, calling on the magic held in its beads. And Emogene always came through. Whether or not the pain subsided, I always had the strength to keep on going. Those Hail Marys were a verbal stim that allowed me to unflex my mind through repetition. So if I let the church go, would I also lose Our Madonna of Emogene?

Don't get me wrong, I always knew my faith was different, but I always believed that I could find a place to exist in the church despite my misgivings. I went to a Jewish preschool, much to my aunts' chagrin, and, as both of my aunts were divorced, had two godmothers. When asked to pray for my future husband at that middle school retreat, I implored Mary to give him the wrong set of directions. And while almost every girl in my Confirmation class chose Saint Thérèse or Saint Cecilia—in my eyes, hyperfeminine figures of divine chastity—I selected Saint Helena, Constantine's mother, who led an expedition to find the True Cross in the Holy Land. Even the bishop confirming me did a double take while reading the little card.

And I grew up in a family whose mom's side had its roots in Appalachian folk magic. My Papa Joe's mom was so Baptist that she even refused to set foot in the church where he and Nonnie were married, furious that Papa Joe had converted to Catholicism. Within her family was a matrilineal line of seers who anticipated any harm or catastrophe for the family. I was told to keep this under wraps at my childhood parish, just like how I took birth control for my severe PCOS. Don't want to give someone the wrong idea. That was just a little family quirk, which I would later learn tied me to a centuries-old tradition of folk magic practiced in the Appalachian Mountains.

So I knew I was different, but I still genuinely believed that my definition of Catholicism, as weird and mystical as it was, grounded in relics, sacramentals, and devotionals—spooky things that satiated little Emma's absolute adoration for Halloween—was valid. But as I grew up and came to understand the church's stance on queer people, I was met with a crossroads. I had been able to rationalize everything else about myself with my Catholic faith—my love of the macabre, my magical view of Emogene's rosary, even my irascible fury at the church's treatment of women throughout its history (a fury I believed Emogene and Mary, the mother of Jesus, shared).

But my sexuality was the one major roadblock. It meant my uncle couldn't fulfill his promise of performing all the Sacraments. It meant that I couldn't baptize any child I had within the church, even though my potential partner and I may have been able to serve as godparents. And, most importantly, it meant that I had to let Emogene go. To me, I was told that being queer meant leaving my religion, denying that any of this was real. It meant denying that objects had power, that Emogene's rosary contained the power of thousands of Hail Marys, ready to whip into action when I needed it most. What happened if I had another panic attack, another bowel-shredding cramp session, or an hour-long attempt at spelunking for a vein? I also inherited Emogene's roly-poly veins—in the end, they put in a shunt because they couldn't keep sticking her.

I now realize that this is a false dichotomy perpetuated both by the church and the LGBTQ+ community, the latter largely because of the intense trauma caused by Christian institutions worldwide. But as someone whose life was built around the church, whose name itself spun stories of divine reincarnation, it felt like life or death. And it felt like I would lose one of the most important people in my life, someone I had never met in person. I share this to acknowledge that many queer people like myself feel the same urgency of "choice" or being pushed to "decide" between living as their authentic selves and drinking the Kool-Aid of the church.

Today, I remain distant from the formal church, but I still carry and pray with Emogene's rosary. Taking a page out of my

Appalachian grandma's book, I have rediscovered folk Catholicism and folk magic as queer-affirming traditions that allow me to reclaim the relics, devotionals, and sacramentals of my childhood. Emogene and Mary are still furious women who fight on my behalf, and God is nonbinary, transcending gender roles and presentations. Angels surround me every night as I picture listening to my mom read the book *Emma and Mommy Talk to God* when I was a child, and for the first time I feel as though I hold within myself a divine power.

Now, it's not one that can bend space and time, as I believed as a child angels could, but it's one that acknowledges that my authentic self is as holy as Emogene's rosary. That through my queerness I am in communion with Christ, with God, with Emogene. I can possess and wield this queerness for good in much the same way that my seven-year-old mind imagined angels could, fighting with a divine fury on earth against church-condoned and -enforced queerphobia. And I am doing it with the same ferocious face that stared down cancer with daggers.

Part Two

BELONGING, BAPTISM, AND ACCEPTANCE

The father, the son, and the I.D.I. spirit

Mack Rogers

I was seventeen when I learned that my spirituality would never resemble that of my parents, specifically my dad. I had been in band or at least playing music since fourth grade. I was to be recognized at Senior Night, the next biggest high school event, in my mom's eyes, after taking a girl I liked to prom. All the seniors from the football team, the cheerleaders, and the marching band were to gather on the field with our parents in front of the whole school. Our names were called over the loudspeaker along with short descriptions of our accomplishments. As a closeted gay, there weren't a lot of spaces in which I felt comfortable being in the spotlight, but this was one of them, so I wanted both my parents to come.

At my single mother's suggestion, I waited to ask Dad until he came to visit the week before. Knowing my dad as a devout Seventh-day Adventist, I knew it was a long shot because it took place during a home game on a Friday evening. His Sabbath started Friday at sunset and ended Sunday at sunrise. But I didn't let that deter me. In the living room, we waited for him among the various Bible-verse wall decals with a different cursive font for each word or phrase plus the more classic crosses and framed Bible verses that hung on the walls. It was a strange occasion for Mom to light the three-wicked cinnamon candle on the coffee table. We'd had that candle for years, and she still has it. I suspected it was because she was just as uncomfortable about meeting with Dad as I was. It was one of his ceremonial visits that I would've preferred to avoid. Both my parents have always preferred to have these conversations in person but especially my dad. Having already been briefed by my mom, he walked in having already prepared to let me down easy.

"I'm sorry, I.D.I.," he told me, as always calling me the nickname he'd given me as a toddler—short for "I do it," which is something I apparently said frequently. "I have to honor the Sabbath. If I were to come, the sun would set before I could get back home."

With my seventeen-year-old logic, I then asked, "Would you come to my funeral if it was held on a Friday evening?"

Without hesitating, he said no. And when I asked him why, he replied, "What would be the point?" while fashioning the sincerest smile I have ever witnessed.

I had always known my dad as an evangelical, but this was the first time I had to reckon with it. Masquerading as a straight man was second nature to me, especially with my parents, but I hadn't realized that we had fundamentally different outlooks on the world until that day.

The concept of different denominations was lost on me and still is even to this day. For much of my time in grade school, my mom and grandma worked at the nursery for a local Episcopal church, and they would bring me along and buy me a McDonald's chicken biscuit for breakfast. Once or twice, I went upstairs for service. It was filled with uncomfortable pews, boring hymns, and sermons that felt like canned vegetables you could have ready to eat in less than five minutes. In and out in an hour tops. But after the parents came down and got their children, we'd always go to our extended family's Black Baptist church. It was a couple blocks up the road at the local community cultural center. As you might imagine, the hymns were not boring and the sermons were always off the cuff—but the pews were still uncomfortable, of course. Sometimes we'd be there three or four hours listening to our cousin compare Martin Luther King Jr. to Jesus in some new way. But Seventh-day Adventists? I never audited their services, and I didn't really feel like I needed to. My dad would show up at our house to give me a nonconsensual sermon at any given time. And yes, even sitting on the couch in my own house, the seating was uncomfortable. It was all simply uncomfortable to me, no matter the location or the length of time.

I'm from Morristown, Tennessee, a small town big enough for a megachurch but too small for a Sam's Club. The blanket of constant religious guilt you get with a close-knit community like Morristown has an added bonus of guilt if you try to move or succeed in moving away. Like most Appalachian communities, there was and still is a sense of contentment with the way things are. And it's a belief shared by most if not all of the older generations that slowly was and still is absorbed by the younger generation. An understood rule was that you didn't leave your family, and by association you didn't leave the church. So I stayed longer than I ought to have, and I was endlessly asked if I got a girlfriend yet. I had been bullied enough, being nerdy and Black, that I didn't entertain the idea of being openly gay for several years. I remained under the city-wide gaydar because of my well-practiced nonverbal response to the casually homophobic comments I heard regularly coupled with references to the Bible. The evangelical sect of Christianity was so ingrained there that you didn't need a direct instance of homophobia to know that it was against the rules. The queer population was almost nonexistent. Luckily, the prejudice I experienced was mostly indirect, but I still didn't bother correcting strangers when they assumed I was straight.

My spiritual beliefs are much more up to interpretation. To put a label on it, I am an agnostic theist. Essentially, I *feel* like there's probably a god or some celestial being that created all this, but I need proof before I'm ready to fully believe it. If I had to pray to a god, it would be the God of Change from Octavia E. Butler's Earthseed series. In my mind, the god that might preside over us all isn't one with rigid rules but one that evolves with us, which is to say my belief system is the antithesis of major organized religions.

Believing in God wasn't really a choice, and neither were the fundamental rules of Christianity. Growing up, I was constantly reminded of the Ten Commandments, the fifth one in particular: the "love your parents" one. At its core, it makes sense. We're all born with this unspoken connection to these two people who helped create us—that is, if we're lucky enough to have both or either of them in our lives. But can we really call it lucky if the burden of maintaining the relationship is put solely on the child? Before my dad started ambushing me with scripture, he would arrange playdates for the two of us. There weren't many things to do within a thirty-minute radius. My dad knew the owner of this hole-in-the-wall theater next to Ingle's, and we'd catch matinees there and hang out in the projector room. He taught me to bowl at West End Lanes, Morristown's bowling alley hidden behind a Cook Out and Taco Bell, in those mandatory shoes you rent. But mostly, he would steal me away to play putt putt at any of the courses within driving distance. We ran out of courses in no time. Honestly, the stuff we did was usually pretty fun, but it quickly became a chore. If I didn't tell the man that I loved him at least twice, he would go back to his home just outside Greeneville, Tennessee, certain that I didn't love him. I would say that on paper this sounds vaguely quintessential for most Appalachian fathers, but my dad had a penchant for voicing that particular concern only to my mother and not directly to me. At least not at the time.

Several years ago, during one of his ambush sermons, we got on the topic of what it means to love. He started out by asking me if I loved him and why. Of course, I said yes because of the support he had given me. We were getting child support, so a lot of the privileges I had were at least in part because of his contribution. I loved him because he cared about me and went to great lengths to show me that he cared about me, though I'm sure I didn't articulate this at the time. I wasn't surprised when he didn't believe me this time either; it was hard for me to say it and really mean it with how preachy he was. For reference, these sermons lasted at least an hour but usually closer to two, and he spoke on his definition of love for quite a while. I sat quietly, listening to him preach, nodding along every so often, talking only when he asked something of me. I hit my breaking point about three-quarters of the way through, and I posed the same question to him that he'd asked of me: did he love me and why. His answer was yes, because God said he had to.

This is the point where I should say that my dad is the nicest person *you'll* ever meet. That's not to say he's not nice to his family, because he is. I think it would be easy to call him overly generous for generosity's sake, but I want to believe it's because he's genuinely a nice guy. My mom pined over him for years, and he answered that love by marrying another woman, but despite that, he still comes around to help whenever she needs it. He'd probably give me money with no strings attached if I asked him to. But my dad follows the Bible almost to the letter. He doesn't eat meat except some seafood, for example, and he always says grace before he eats, which may as well be a sermon itself. I couldn't tell you if that's actually in the Bible, but I feel like it must be since his life is structured around that text. I never gave the Bible much of my attention, but learning that he had married twice, with neither woman being my mother, totally skewed my understanding of right and wrong from a Christian point of view.

That's generally been my experience with Christianity—being told that I'm not living the right way with virtually zero real-life examples of what that looks like. And asking why, in regard to the Bible, while not necessarily discouraged, is a losing battle. I wasn't supposed to ask why my dad loved me in the same way I wasn't supposed to ask why my cousins tried to push me to the floor while they were speaking in tongues around me after coercing me into an altar call. This was how they worshipped, and some things, no matter how extreme, were nonnegotiable. Maybe somewhere in that book it says all these things are normal, and if they can find even one sentence that says as much, there's no point in arguing it.

My relationship with the commercialized God was already on thin ice before Senior Night. I was never given a choice in the matter when it came to my religious beliefs. I knew I was gay when I was seven or eight, but I didn't come to fully accept that until I was twenty-five. When I was a child, anytime I had a homosexual thought, I would frantically recite a prayer under my breath, begging God to forgive me while furiously rebuking Satan. I had gathered that as long as you ask for forgiveness, everything would come out in the wash, but I wasn't sure why I was saying sorry—I was just certain that I should. I later learned that this was where my issues with Christianity began to intersect with my father. Both had this frustrating habit of being unable or unwilling to give me a decent explanation for why something is to be believed, which is probably why I was terrified of him ever finding out that I was gay. He was never one to explicitly ask if I had a girlfriend or hint at having grandchildren, but he was always so righteously obedient to the Bible. Perhaps his sermons were because he had his suspicions, but even if he had good gaydar, he wasn't around enough to make an educated guess. I was a different person around him, so I suspect his sermons were fueled more by my lack of spirituality than my homosexuality. Unless my mom had planted the seed in his head, which, frankly, wouldn't have been out of character for her.

Mom claimed to know I was gay when I got hemorrhoids in college, which is hilarious only because I wasn't having sex then. She confessed this while I was coming out to her in October 2019, but I like to think she said it only to lighten the mood. There's simply no way she didn't know way before that. We may have never talked about it, but I got a virus on our shared computer from gay porn. And seeing as she had this "there's no secrets among family" ideology, it wouldn't surprise me if she had confided in most of my family about my potential gayness. Though I suspect having a girl best friend whose house I would go to constantly threw her a bit. Regardless, my mom was and is supportive. She still sometimes refers to my partner as my friend around family, but baby steps, ya know?

I met my partner in November 2019, just a month after I had the talk with my mom, and along with his group of queer or queer-adjacent friends, I found myself in a sort of queer microcosm in Johnson City. I was still living with Mom in Morristown at the time and would drive up on the weekends. In June 2020 I made a Facebook/blog post to come out publicly, which was purely ceremonial (and to air my grievances surrounding the death of George Floyd, but that's another essay). The way I saw it, the only person in my life who deserved hearing it face to face was my mom. And so I told her to tell whoever she felt like telling. My dad fell in that category. We still talked at the time but rarely. Mom would goad me into calling him on his birthday and on Father's Day and to send him a card every year. I'd see him on the holidays or at least call him. But somehow he always made it out to seem like it was my fault that we didn't talk, even though he called my mom pretty often and there was only a wall separating us. Even after my mom told him I was gay, the message she conveyed to me was simply "he wants you to call him, I think you'll be surprised," which I took to mean that he was either accepting or didn't care that I was gay. But I put my foot down. I'd made it clear to Mom that I didn't care about hiding or acceptance anymore; the only person I needed to accept me was her. If he had something to say, why couldn't he pick up the phone?

By fall of 2020 my partner and I had broken up (which lasted only a couple of months before we got back together), so all of my time was spent at home with Mom. It gave me a lot of time to reflect on what really mattered to me and where I was going in life, and I concluded that I wanted to go to grad school. At the time, I worked at a bank with strict COVID policies that meant even close contact with someone who had tested positive meant two weeks of paid leave. I'm not proud of it, but since I had decided to go back to school to study creative writing less than a month before most schools' application deadlines, I took advantage of the situation and earned myself two weeks of personal time to get my materials together. I faked contact with a friend who had tested positive. In the spirit of full transparency, I confessed this to my mom. I felt like I ought to, seeing as I was living with her, and she was bound to find out anyway. Remember how I said my mom and dad talked over the phone often?

Yeah, well, she told him, which I have to believe she thought was totally harmless. So in the middle of editing my submission for the fourth time, there was a knock at the door. It was my dad.

This was the first time he'd had an actual reason to show up unannounced and the first time I'd seen him since coming out. To be perfectly honest, I thought he had come to talk to me about my homosexuality, but of course he came to berate me for lying to get out of work. It wasn't in his nature to come with an olive branch or acknowledge things that didn't make sense to him. I reluctantly led him back to the same living room, mostly unchanged in the past ten years, and I folded myself into the love seat. He sat across from me. He thought what I had done—what I was doing—was wrong, and I mean I didn't have much room to argue with him because I was fully aware of the immorality of that decision. Nevertheless, I got a sermon, which, if I'm being honest, was kind of a blur, but it was mostly reminding me of my obligation to work and Bible verses to back up that claim.

I tended to zone out during sermons, not exclusively my father's. By then my ability to stare and nod while maintaining the illusion of listening was unmatched, but he caught me at a really bad time. The breakup was still fresh, but the wound at that time was gradually closing, and I was devoting much of my energy to repairing what I'd lost emotionally on top of being immensely stressed with writing. Really, there was never going to be a suitable time for my dad to do this, but I humored him for a few minutes anyway before I started boiling over.

"Why are you doing this?" I asked during his next brief pause.

"I'm trying to get you back on the right path," he said. "To help remind you of the difference between right and wrong."

"Dad, I know what I'm doing isn't necessarily right, but I'm only doing it so I can get my grad school application materials ready in time. Mom must have told you that."

"I do understand, I.D.I., but that doesn't make it right."

I broke down. "You can't keep doing this, Dad. I'm an adult," I said. I sobbed as I paced in front of the door. "I don't know what I'm doing. But somehow, I finally have direction in my life. I am willing to risk my job if it means that I can get one step closer to the life I've always imagined for myself. After all that therapy, I am finally rediscovering having real joy in my life. This past year was the happiest I've ever been. I was in love, I made new friends, and I am happy being myself for the first time. And I was even happy right up until you came in here with your usual shit."

And with a straight face he said, "I.D.I., you're not happy."

I took those four words as *the way you are living your life is wrong*. It was the fact that he wouldn't even acknowledge any of the good things in my life, specifically being an out gay man, that threw me over the edge. Despite my resentment toward him, I wanted him to be proud of me. But in that moment, I knew that I would never be a success in his eyes. It felt like, as he and many other Christians have put it, I was born a sinner and would always be one.

But can you understand how confounding a statement that is? I wasn't happy? First of all, my dad and I are wildly different people. How could he consider himself the leading authority on whether I was happy? I saw him maybe only four or five times a year. We spoke only on holidays or when he figured I needed to be read to from the Bible. I couldn't think of anyone less qualified in my family to speak on my emotional state than him, and I was a pretty closed-off person when I interacted with my family already for reasons you may be able to guess. Happiness, to him, wasn't something you could achieve without God, which put us at an impasse.

I realized then that I would always be a child in my dad's eyes. I mean, he still called me by my toddler nickname. And the irony of that nickname. I do it, but only if God says it's OK. I do it, but not very well. There were a lot more don'ts than do's when it came to Christianity and my father. He must've felt solely responsible for the void of spirituality in my life and that only he could fill it. This wasn't the man who used to whisk me away to an indeterminate bonding activity practically every time he saw me. Or maybe it was.

All the taking me to movies, bowling, and putt putt were, after all, mostly impersonal affairs. We were almost always late for the movies, and we would always get too competitive for bonding when we bowled or played mini golf. He was certain that I didn't love him because he didn't give me a reason to love him apart from financial support and the occasional coerced bonding ritual. His version of "I do it" was doing exactly as I was told. That is the core of our dysfunction. I'll never be able to love my dad the way he wants to be loved, and he's offended by that. And he loves me because that's what it says in the Bible.

I do have fond memories of times with my father, but it's hard not to see those moments as performative when juxtaposed with the surprise come-to-Jesus talks that dominated our tumultuous relationship. They're the times he chaperoned on school trips when he would pick up my friends and carry them on his shoulders. Or the time he came to Honors Night in middle school and shouted "that one's mine" when I got recognized. I never quite understood why he was like a totally different person around other people until that day he told me I wasn't happy. It was the fact that I cited my queerness and my self-discovery as the primary contributors to my happiness that demolished any semblance of a common ground between us. But rather than earnestly listen to me, he instead chose to persist in his efforts to change me.

"Get out," I said. "Get out of my house." I have never been so fueled by rage as I was that day.

"This isn't your house. It's your momma's," he said.

"It's more my house than it will ever be yours. Now, get out."

Years later, I'm still waiting on that apology. And he's still waiting on mine, I suppose. I later learned from my mom after she invited me to a family get-together that maybe bringing my partner wasn't the best idea—because my dad would be there. I've spoken to him a couple of times since then when my mom has called me to talk and then—surprise—"your daddy's here too." He's taken to calling me "Mackenzie" now. She has said explicitly that she still wants me to have a relationship with my father. My heavenly father, at least.

Remembering Your Baptism in Appalachia: A Queer Christian's Manifesto

John Golden

I do not actually remember my baptism. And, though I now claim Appalachia as my home, I moved here only in May 2018. And yet I believe that the land has laid a claim on me; the land sparks a memory that I previously forgot or had never truly known; Appalachia reminds me of rebirth and renewal, of sacrament and spirituality, of connection, of life, and of death.

I was baptized as an infant. I received the sacrament of baptism at my grandparents' Methodist church in Texarkana, Texas. A few years ago, my mom mailed me my baptismal certificate, and I keep it lovingly in my office, on a shelf with other memorabilia that tells a symbolic narrative of who I am.

While "believer's baptism" feels like the more normative experience for many of the Christians I have met, infant baptism is an important part of my personal Christian tradition. I was raised within a particular flavor of Christianity known as the Reformed Tradition, or, as some people call it, Calvinism. This tradition is a major branch of Christianity, breaking away from the Roman Catholic Church in the sixteenth century to protest some of the malpractices within the church.

At its best, the Reformed Tradition affirms that God has always loved us, will always love us, and loves us right now. That God's love is always present in our lives. That God's grace is unconditional, unearned, and undeserved. Infant baptism represents this theological stance by sharing this sacrament with a person prior to any confession of faith, prior to any conscious action.

Infant baptism is witnessed by a congregation, the Body of Christ, which affirms this person as another member of that Body. During an infant baptism, the minister will turn to the congregation and ask, "Do you, as members of the church of Jesus Christ, promise to guide and nurture them, by word and deed, with love and prayer, encouraging them to know and follow Christ and to be faithful members of Christ's church?" At that moment, the pastor is implicitly asking the congregation to remember their baptism. They are called to remember that they are loved by Christ, a love that is experienced through other members of the Body of Christ who likewise promised to guide, nurture, and encourage the members of the congregation. The foremost way a church remembers our baptism is witnessing the baptism of others.

❧

There is something queerly erotic about the ritual of baptism.

In the Gospel of Matthew, Jesus approaches John, propositioning him, "Will you baptize me?" Will you immerse my body into the water, and let your gospel of repentance and love penetrate my soul? John responds, "I need to be baptized by you, yet you come to me?" Surely you ought to be the one immersing me, for your capacity for love-making is bigger than mine. Jesus answers, "Allow me to be baptized now. This is necessary to fulfill all righteousness." Let me be the one immersed. I need this to know the fullness of the human experience. John consents to this proposition. Though Jesus was expected to take on the role of a top for this ritual, for his own baptism, he opened himself up as a bottom.

Jesus is plunged into the river Jordan. The shorelines are spread apart like two legs, and the muddy wetness of the Jordan flows through them. Jesus convulses; the euphoria of being surrounded in body and spirit by the creature that you love ripples through Christ's body. Then the Christ emerges from the water, enraptured, aglow with ecstasy and dripping with dew. In that moment of transcendental, joyful release, the clouds part ways. Many medieval art pieces portray a vulva-like wound in Christ's side during his crucifixion; could the clouds parting ways likewise be imagined as the opening of God's womb? The Jordan River, the amniotic fluid of Christ's new birth? The dove resting upon Christ, the very mark of God's dear love and abundant happiness?

I was raised in a culturally conservative area with a culturally conservative family. And as a queer person who internalized those ideologies for far too long, I have not always felt comfortable in my body. The expectations and behaviors and performances that are assigned to my "male" body are not in full congruence with my own expectations, behaviors, or manners that direct my performances. Baptism makes a spiritual claim: Hegemony no longer has a claim on my body. Those destructive, reductionist, essentialist claims to my identity no longer have any hold upon me. Instead, I am remade and re-created with and within a body that I love and that is beloved.

My journey to East Tennessee was never part of my plan. I moved here in May 2018, after enrolling at Emmanuel Christian Seminary. I had entertained the thought of going into ministry when I was in high school, as church events and religious spaces and experiences within the Christian body were where I felt the strongest sense of belonging. However, I ignored those thoughts for two primary reasons: pursuing my idea of the American dream, and the secret that I feared invalidated my sense of call: my queer identity.

My desire to acquire wealth, power, and prestige—the American dream!—waned throughout my undergraduate program. I was a competent but never excellent engineering student. After the second year in my program, I was hired to work as an engineering intern for three semesters, alternating semesters between work and academic studies. I worked for a company with a large manufacturing plant in Augusta, Georgia. As I worked adjacent to manufacturing workers, measuring efficiencies, counting defective products, conducting time studies, and demanding increased performance, I became disillusioned at the lack of humanity within this system. The corporation was a body that consumed bodies. Employment was conditional upon production, production was perpetually insufficient, and insufficiencies had to be identified and eliminated. The people with power and prestige were never the ones eliminated; they were unwilling to disburse their wealth to address inefficiencies; the manufacturing workers at the bottom of the pay scale were the most disposable. By the time I graduated from undergrad, my burgeoning class consciousness meant I no longer had any interest in working as a cog for the corporate machine.

However, I was not yet ready to commit to pursuing a vocation in ministry. I was still nonaffirming of my queer identity, and I needed to prove to myself that my queer identity would not be a liability to a ministerial vocation. After graduating, I participated in a gap-year program and worked as an intern at a nondenominational campus ministry in Atlanta, Georgia. For the first month I worked there, I felt like I belonged in this evangelical setting.

This sense was shattered on September 16, 2017, when Scout Schultz was shot and killed by an officer of the Georgia Tech Police Department. Scout was a fourth-year computer engineering major and the president of the Pride Alliance at Georgia Tech. After an investigation, authorities announced that this was a suicide by cop and that the police overreacted to a person in obvious mental distress. Scout was nonbinary, the first nonbinary person I ever became aware of. Nonbinary—just like I am.

LGBTQ+ people began attending the nondenominational campus ministry in increased numbers and in increased visibility that year, seeking spiritual comfort after that devastating tragedy. And yet, I found myself avoiding them. Though I could abstractly affirm their gender and sexual identity, I still could not yet affirm mine. If I validated their queerness, then I would have to validate my own as well. And at that time, I could not. My cognitive dissonance marginalized me from both my queer body and that evangelical Christian body. I could not offer pastoral presence to those seeking it, and I felt like a failure.

At the end of the gap-year program, one of the campus ministers encouraged me to pursue ministry anyway. Plenty of pastors have struggled with sin in their lives and been effective ministers of the gospel. Paul himself had a thorn in his flesh that tormented him throughout his ministry, according to his second letter to the Corinthians. "Give yourself a little grace," the campus minister told me. With that small amount of grace given, and with that small amount received, I moved to Johnson City the next week to attend seminary, to discover my voice in ministry, and to wade into a trickling stream of grace.

A month after I moved to East Tennessee, on a warm and sunny June day, I was invited to join three women to go on a rafting adventure down the Nolichucky River. Sarah and Kimberly were beginning their second year of seminary; Anna was enrolling in seminary that fall, just as I was. We traveled down I-26, got off at exit 40, and shuttled ourselves upriver to a parking spot. We then walked along the train tracks, looking for a point to launch. We entered the water and began floating down the river, nestled between the beautiful green hills of Appalachia.

At some point during the float, Anna began talking about her upbringing as a missionary kid, her experience as a student at a Bible college, and her journey with reconciling her sexuality as a lesbian. Although her story was distinctly different from mine, I remember thinking and feeling that there were a remarkable number of similarities between us. The most significant difference between us, at that moment, was that she was affirming her queer identity and I was not; she had reconciled her queer identity and her Christian faith, and I had not.

And so, in the cold, flowing, living waters of the Nolichucky, my mind was transformed. I entered the river that day in denial about myself. I emerged from the river affirming the gender and sexuality and identity that God had graciously and lovingly formed within my very being. My journey toward queer acceptance, queer affirmation, queer validation, had plunged forward.

In one of the historical theology classes I took in seminary, the professor presented a lecture on baptism to the class. He described how, at some confluence of time and space within the Christian tradition, a priest would walk into the river or other flowing body of water with the person seeking to be baptized. After the person seeking baptism had made their profession of faith, the priest would begin the baptism. "In the name of the Father," the priest intoned before grabbing their head and violently dunking them under the water. The priest would hold them there, squirming and struggling underwater, until he finally raised them up. "In the name of the Son," the priest intoned before again grabbing the person's head and holding them underwater. Bubbles would rise, and the water would churn, the person seeking baptism fighting against drowning. The person was raised again, gasping for breath, for precious air. "In the name of the Holy Spirit," the megalomaniacal priest would say before plunging the person seeking baptism one last time. Finally, the priest would raise the person up a third time. Their initiation into the Christian body was concluded.

The church historian, with his own megalomaniacal disposition, would smirk at the discomfort felt by the students as he described this violent method of celebrating baptism. "Baptism," he said, "is a symbol of our burial with Jesus into death and our resurrection with Christ from death. But baptism is also a powerful symbol of our dependence on God to breathe new life into us. We are buried with Christ, we are raised in Christ, and we are dependent upon Christ for the very breath we breathe and the inbreaking of the Holy Spirit in that breath."

During my first year in Appalachia, I worked as a lab technician for a construction laboratory. I tested concrete and soil at construction sites all throughout Northeast Tennessee and Southwest Virginia. If you look at my Google Maps, you can see pins marking all the places I traveled to assess the foundations of various construction projects. I occasionally joked that this job would at least provide one good sermon illustration if I ever chose to preach on "building the church on the rock." Working as a lab technician did more than that—it was the context in which my newly emerging queer identity felt like it was drowning the most.

Every place I had previously lived—East Texas, Atlanta, and Augusta—has its fair share of people struggling through poverty and beholden to bigotry. But while I was "slinging concrete," I entered a strange intimacy and communion with people who had lower educational attainment, came from less privileged socioeconomic backgrounds, and held on to bigoted ideologies. As I worked alongside these people who professed racist, sexist, homophobic, transphobic, and xenophobic viewpoints, my body thrashed as if it were underwater, experiencing the weightiness of those suffocating ideologies.

One day, I traveled to a job site to test the soil and concrete at the location of some future apartment buildings. They were in their early stage of development. On that gray, wintry day I approached the foreman, a man with a persona beyond caricature. The foreman was a grizzled, cigar-chomping mountain of a man; he watched closely as I tested for soil compaction. I matched his gruff demeanor, mirroring his macho toughness as best as I could. I drove the T-rod into the ground, plunging it deep into the rocky soil. I pounded the soil with the sledge compactor with extra vigor, sneering at him when I shared the results of the tests.

I felt his eyes drilling holes into my back as I worked. Though I was masked in pseudo-masculinity, I could not mask my ponytail, bobbing in the wind. I prayed that this burly man would not see that as a marker of the effeminate person I truly am. I prayed that I would not be outed as a genderfluid femme-boy who had entered an ecstatic joy while twirling around in a dress to the tune of bluegrass music the weekend before. I prayed in gratitude that I had elected not to wear a sports bra to work that day, though it would not be visible through the layers of clothes I was wearing. I prayed imprecatory prayers, wielding them as my silent weapon, my only line of defense, against this man who made me feel so vulnerable in my body.

Sometime while I was there, I told him that I was enrolled in seminary, studying theology, and so we got to talking about religion and politics. The foreman looked me dead in the eye and told me, "All Democrats are damned to hell!" I asked him, "Now what makes you so sure of that?" He replied that because Democratic party leadership affirmed abortion access, all who voted for the Democratic party implicitly endorsed abortion and were therefore going to hell. I was riled up at his attack, so I accused him in turn: "Oh yeah? Well, I think all Republicans are going to hell!" I then pointed to the human rights abuses occurring on the Mexican border at the hands of the Republican administration and how the people who elected those officials were culpable for those abuses by his logic. We both huffed and puffed at one another, exchanging toxic machismo blow for blow.

I got home late that night and began reading for seminary: *Just Mercy*, by Bryan Stephenson. As I turned the pages, my mind turned between my reflections on the death penalty and on the interaction with the grizzly man. Eventually, I began to break down, so I put down my pen, crawled into bed, and cried myself to sleep. The gravity of the theological statement I had uttered earlier that day hit me: I had told this man from the hollers of Appalachia that because of the ballots he had cast, I thought that he was removed from the grace of God. I had forgotten my baptismal vows; I had forgotten the grace of God; I had buried him in sin.

Sometimes, affirming myself and integrating my faith and identity have felt like the most natural things in the world. Floating the Nolichucky, my heart felt unburdened by the years of self-hatred I had internalized. God's unconditional love felt more real for myself and for all other queer folk. Unconditional love extended to me, and unconditional love extended to everyone and everything.

Affirming my queer identity and integrating it within Christian faith while living in these mountains has also, at times, felt like the violent sort of baptism that my church history professor taught us about. I felt like I was drowning that night. The vitriol that sputtered out from me that day emerged from a deep woundedness. The years of poisonous faith I had professed throughout my conservative evangelical experiences had not yet been exorcized fully from my body, and they may never be. Many people may experience this whiplash.

Remembering our baptism reminds us of two things: We remember that each one of us is within the Body of Christ, beloved by God, and we remember that those to whom God's grace extends beyond ourselves are also beloved by God. God's grace extends both to God's covenant people, those who practice righteousness, and to those on opposite ideological lines from us.

For those who have been oppressed, traumatized, or victimized, it may be excruciatingly painful to affirm that God's grace may still extend to the one who has caused them harm. And I do so with trepidation. But I do so with the lens of my experiences. I have seen Appalachia satirized by Hollywood and spoken of in demeaning ways by authors such as JD Vance. I have encountered what the *New York Times* calls "Trump's America" and the people that Hillary Clinton labeled the "basket of deplorables." I have encountered the homophobia, misogyny, racism, and bigotry that is pervasive throughout Appalachia and that I had likewise internalized and embodied for much of my life; I full-heartedly condemn all these expressions of bigotry.

But in my time in Appalachia, I have come to see these issues as symptoms of larger problems. To reduce it to its smallest essence, the problem Appalachia experiences is the power imbalances that lead to the exploitation of the land and the people. Relational violence ripples from this capital sin, leading to the fragmentation of peoples and creation. Some of the most bigoted people I have encountered have never received nurturing and guidance in word and deed, love and prayer, from the people they have developed resentment toward. The cycle of relational violence can be interrupted, paused for the briefest of moments, if the two parties can simultaneously remember their baptism and their mutual belovedness by God. If we condemn the bigotry of others without critically examining our own dehumanizing practices, we risk condemning ourselves. If we distance ourselves from those who have been impoverished the most from colonizing, imperialistic exploitation of the land, then we divorce ourselves from people who are most in need.

I am not saying that we should place any of our vulnerable, traumatized, injured bodies into places where they could be reinjured or traumatized again. But what I am saying is that we should remember that we are a part of the same body. We drink water that flows down the same mountain streams. We eat food grown from the same soil. We abide in a world that is increasingly affected by climate change. We live under a plutocracy that increasingly hordes wealth. We suffer the same ill effects of shared existence together. But if we can live together in closer harmony, reconciling ourselves to one another, perhaps we can experience the health and healing of Appalachia, and our world, together.

Theologian Sally McFague writes, "We are not separate, static, individuals. . . . On the contrary, we belong from the cells of our bodies to the finest creations of our minds, to the intricate, constantly changing cosmos. The ecosystem of which we are part is a whole: the rocks and waters, atmosphere and soil, plants, animals, and human beings interact in dynamic, mutually supportive ways. . . . Relationships and interdependence, change and transformation, are how we must function." By holding to this belief, I remember my baptism; when I remember my baptism, I am witness to the baptismal belovedness of all. I remember all this when I remember my baptism in Appalachia.

Testimony

Chelsea Bock

In the summer of 2011, a photographer at a western Maryland gay bar captures me in a moment of dance floor bliss. Fitted in black hot pants, knee-high pleather boots, something between a shirt and a vest, and a studded bra I bought at the behest of a friend who loved it but would never wear it herself, I recline against the girl I came out here to see. My hand grazes her thigh while she whispers something into my neck. We're both laughing and raising our drinks. Queer joy radiates from our bodies, the pulse of the blue stage lights, the men chatting excitedly behind us.

What the photographer doesn't capture is where I've come from and where I'll return to on Monday. My employer, the town evangelical school.

Jobs were hard to come by at the end of my college days. Part of this was basic geography—it's much easier to find something in your field in DC or Baltimore than in the Appalachian counties. But my classmates and I had also graduated into a global financial crisis. Even though I had spent a lot of time working on two majors to maximize my employability, I had seen the people filing out of Lehman Brothers on the evening news and the crop of foreclosure signs on back road properties. I knew what I was up against.

To fulfill a senior year practicum requirement, I interned at a private school not far from where I had grown up. Every Friday I headed over the mountains to a community with a population of a few hundred, its land dotted with churches and Mennonite-owned shops, handmade signs that boasted "Fresh

Squash" and "Baby Bunnies 4 Sale." The campus sat about a half mile back from the main road next to a field of brown grazing cows, but the school itself was a modern build less than ten years old. I learned as much as I could from my supervisor. She was young, fun to be around, and eager to swap college stories and new makeup finds until the day of her resignation.

"Get in here," she said, hustling me into her office. "Close the door."

I had my little notebook with me, as always, but this wasn't a little notebook kind of day.

"I asked them to hire you as my replacement. They'll need someone, and you graduate in a month. It's perfect."

Perfect was a stretch. I knew that I didn't fit in but also that it hadn't mattered much because of how infrequent my presence was. My longest conversation with another staff member was necessitated by a project for my Advanced Reporting class, a feature piece comparing the sex education curricula of a private and a public school. "Break God's laws? I don't see that in the Bible," the teacher explained of the school's abstinence-only approach during our interview. "I'd rather students didn't know about all that." I dictated and tried not to wince. More hours on campus meant more blending in on my part and inevitably higher expectations on theirs.

"Do you think they'll accept me?" I asked as much to myself as to my supervisor.

"I want to show you something," she said, crossing the room. "Look out there in the lobby. I could close my eyes, point to any of these people, and bet there's something they wouldn't want you to know." My supervisor turned around and rested her hands on my shoulders. "Everyone has their secrets. I'm sure you have yours too."

Suddenly I was coordinating fundraisers, school assemblies, special family days, and even the annual auction. I would be making hourly pay and wouldn't have my own health insurance. But it was much more than most of my cohort had lined up, and despite the looming challenges I was grateful. There was a quaintness to the area that had made my weekly drives so pleasurable—could I focus on that? The ice cream parlor, the horseback riding stables, the white farmhouse with every color truck lined up in the driveway like Skittles. Wasn't it supposed to be hard to feel stressed in a place like this?

After my supervisor moved on, one of the principals took her office and I was assigned to a desk behind a barrier in the mailroom. Just like my paycheck and my profile on the school website, the space was mine, and I made it my own. I set up my combination CD player and radio beside the computer and brought in a few pictures of my dogs. The staff that came in to check their mail regarded me quietly until one of the elementary school teachers, hearing me lift boxes, peeped around the partition. "Might want to cover up," she said grimly, gesturing to my blouse. My hand rose to my chest. "Your neckline," she said. "You don't want to give the boys a show." As I straightened up, the headmaster entered.

The headmaster was a tall, white-haired man with a round face and a friendly mustache. He could have been my grandfather, and given the family-oriented nature of the school, it was safe to assume that he was *somebody's* grandfather. He sat in the chair between the doorframe and my desk and presented me with a stack of papers. "These are so we can know more about your Christian life," he said warmly. Internally, I panicked. *Christian life?* The last vaguely Christian thing I had done was eat an entire can of Spam thanks to some weird initiation ritual in my former youth group, and I had told my parents that I wasn't interested in going to any more meetings. (Later, as I sat down to write, I would describe my youth group experience as "less than desirable.")

"It's important that we know more about your commitment to Jesus Christ," the headmaster explained. "That's why we'd like you to write your own testimony chronicling these experiences. You know, when you were born again, what Bible-based church you go to. Things like that." More panic. *I was already baptized!* I thought. *One and done!* I made a note to look up "Bible-based church" after the headmaster left. Didn't all Christian churches use the Bible? My discomfort and confusion were palpable, but I thanked the headmaster for the information and gathered up my homework. *Okay. You can write this testimony. You've been to enough churches. Say that you're still looking for one. Shit, but then they'll invite you. See if they'll give you a pass for not being born again. Baptized should be good enough. They have to like Lutherans, right? That feels safe. They're Protestants too. Oh, and no more V-necks.*

On the way out of the office, the headmaster bumped the stack of CDs on my desk. "Sting?" he asked before examining the track listing. "'Desert Rose'? 'Fields of Gold'?"

And no more secular music.

Later that week, after reviewing the school's statement of faith and working through my Christian testimony, I spread the policies and procedures manual for staff out on my bedroom carpet. A lot of the material was standard: Teachers should maintain organized and accessible classrooms; students must have a note from home in order to miss school. Some were unexpected and foreign to me: Mornings are led with pledges to both the American flag and the Christian flag; staff members should believe that their work is spiritually led. When in Rome, yeah? It would be unreasonable for me to expect the perfect match from my first job after college.

But as I read, the manual morphed from guidelines on conduct during school and related events to an uncompromising profile of the person who should grace these halls. "Staff members must agree to be role models in Christian living" was one of the conditions of employment, which specified "refraining from such activities as the use of alcoholic beverages." I finished my glass of wine and grabbed an old Bible from my bookshelf to look up the accompanying verse—for every hard and fast rule, there were multiple verses listed beside it. No tobacco use, no vulgarity, and then I saw the clause that punched me in the stomach.

"Staff members must agree that the unique roles of the male and female are clearly defined in Scripture, and that Romans 1:24–32 condemns the homosexual lifestyle."

There were more verses that followed, presumably to elaborate. I shut the Bible.

By the end of the manual, I learned not only that the school categorically opposed same-sex attraction and relationships but that staff could be fired for engaging in them. "Any sexual misconduct including but not limited to premarital, extramarital, or homosexual activity . . . violates the employment requirement of being a Christian role model," another clause read. Under the section labeled Termination, "homosexual activities" was listed as grounds for any staff member to be "discharged immediately and pay terminated."

I turned in the other requested documents, but for the duration of my employment I kept the unsigned manual in one of my desk drawers. The headmaster never asked about it, and I never mentioned it again. Really, I had to laugh. An angry booklet wasn't going to bring down all the years I'd worked to love myself.

What did it mean to live "the homosexual lifestyle"? Was I living it through my crushes and flirtations, the nights spent at my best friend's house because he was the only one who understood? At first queerness was something that *happened* to me, like a wave rolling in. But over time I would choose it again and again.

When I told the French horn player who had been eyeing me across the band room that I'd go on a date with him, I was unprepared for the displacement I'd feel once he put his head on my shoulder and took my hand. There was a girl I couldn't stop thinking about, but there were also rules. And like every other high school student, I learned those rules by assessing my peers' reactions. Don't kiss another girl after class on the conductor's podium—everyone makes it a big deal. Don't take another girl to prom—the rumors will start, and the questions will be incessant. Keep your hair long so that you won't get called a dyke, and when you watch *The O.C.* at your neighbor's, contain your excitement when Alex kisses Marissa on the beach. This is a Mormon household. She'll never invite you over again.

Church wasn't much better since my parents had recently switched congregations. The pastor there had been a longtime friend of our extended family, and after hearing him give a guest sermon one Sunday, my mom was sold. I liked this pastor. He was small and jovial. As much a counselor as he was a clergyman, he gave advice on major life issues that went far beyond platitudes and resonated days after we spoke. But after each service ended, an uneasiness accompanied the expectation that I would get involved in the church in other ways. A parent in our Sunday school class had pivoted to a post-9/11 pattern of disparaging Muslims and met my mom's angry phone call with a rapid-fire sequence of scriptures before the receiver clicked. The youth group observed a strict hierarchy, and a lot of the teens—mostly members of the more prominent families—were quick to ostracize anyone different. Other than Marissa and Alex from *The O.C.*, I knew only one person who was attracted to multiple genders. He came out as transgender much later in life, but at church he was unapologetically queer and goth and sported the kind of hair I'd previously seen only in anime. He was also made fun of so much on the annual retreat that one of the chaperones suggested, "If you just try to fit in more, maybe the kids will be nicer." I felt God in the gentle pastor's words on Sundays but nowhere else in that building. I would have to answer these questions about myself quietly, kicking up the least amount of fuss.

Every day I woke up committed to figuring out what I was and why. It was a secret project that I would have to work on carefully and certainly not at church, which meant mostly during my time alone or in online forums. My best friend came out to me as gay during our sophomore year, which brought us even closer together, but at the same time I struggled to articulate my own sexuality back to him because I hadn't really seen it represented anywhere. I wanted to drop anchor. If I could just name and understand what I felt, maybe there would eventually be a space where other people would too.

When I was sixteen my mom took me to see *The Hours*, the adaptation of Michael Cunningham's novel about three queer women whose lives intertwine: author Virginia Woolf, '50s housewife Laura Brown reading Woolf's *Mrs. Dalloway*, and Clarissa Vaughn, a twenty-first-century Clarissa Dalloway. Virginia Woolf was one of my favorite writers, and I was fortunate enough to meet my then-girlfriend in a forum for fans of her work and *The Hours* more specifically. "You're the Sally to my Clarissa," I sighed dreamily over the phone one evening, temporarily pushing away the reality that Clarissa and Sally don't end up together in the book. I wanted that young love, that "most exquisite moment," and I wanted it with her. When my mom and I left the theater, I was shaking with sobs. The movie had smashed open a truth I could no longer deny.

On summer vacation that year I cried in the shower almost every day. This was another thing that I had to hide to avoid raising any questions, so I bit down on a washcloth to muffle the sound. I was furious at God for making me this way, a way that would be scorned and misunderstood and "dealt with" unless I kept it tightly under wraps. My girlfriend was supportive, but she was also out to everyone in her much more progressive town and didn't receive regular warnings that she'd be going to hell. The god her family and friends worshiped seemed to love and value everyone. So I tried asking that god, instead of the one people used to excuse their fear of anyone different, if I would ever find peace. I didn't see how being true to myself could be a sin.

After my first relationship with a girl dissolved, I found queer chosen family in the unlikeliest of places. One of my friends from high school started attending my church, and in an effort to try youth events again, I accompanied him to a weekly live music café for teens. Unfortunately, the only thing I got out of going to that café was confirmation that I was still attracted to guys. I don't know what made Paul* turn around in the doorway one afternoon and kiss me so hard on the mouth I saw stars. But once he did, our entire dynamic changed. We snuggled up to each other in history class to complete the day's assignments. In the computer lab he'd rock me back and forth in his arms as we shared a set of headphones and sang along to Bob Marley. We made out at house parties and in the car after late-night trips to West Virginia. It was certainly the safest and most loved I'd ever felt with a boy. It also felt strangely *right* in a way that none of my other opposite-sex relationships had.

One night during our senior year, we went to listen to our songwriting teacher's band perform at a roadside bar across the state line. Our Marlboro Menthol smoke hovered in the

---

* Name changed for privacy.

darkness and mingled with the other patrons' as we ordered some dinner to justify our underage presence. We watched our teacher belt out covers with aplomb—a couple of young old souls admiring the woman with Stevie Nicks hair and style who taught us that it all starts with three chords.

After the band packed up, Paul suggested a night drive down back roads. The conversation wasn't simple. It was like an excavation, and when I got home, I would need to take stock of what was left.

"Is there anyone you have feelings for?" he asked. "At school or church?"

"I'm seventeen. I have feelings for everyone." I laughed.

"That's not an answer."

I stared out the window as we passed a tack shop, then down at his legs. Maybe we could just pull over somewhere and make out again.

"I think I know," he said. "I think it's the same person as me."

My eyes flew open. "*Paul.*"

He shrugged. "I mean, it's always the three of us sitting apart from everyone else. In our own little world. Just you, me, and him."

"Wait," I said. "But we—"

"I think I'm bisexual," he said.

So THAT'S what it's called!

"I'm so glad you said that," I said, squeezing his hand. "I think I am too."

From that night on, our time together gave me a different sense of safety. I could define myself and take up space in something real, not a muddled question between gay and straight. We were two queer kids kissing and chattering about the same boy. And knowing that whatever the future had in store, we'd look out for each other.

In 2009 our church, after many arguments within the congregation, split due to a change in its policies on LGBTQ members and clergy. Paul and I both stopped going, recognizing that God is present wherever someone walks through the door as they are and no one tells them that they don't belong.

I think of this as the real story, the one I couldn't turn in. My Christian testimony.

⊱❦⊰

Despite every effort to be nondescript, I drew plenty of attention during my three years of working at the Christian school. I had gone to public grade school and then to a secular college that, according to one aggrieved parent volunteer, disqualified me from hosting the annual Christian college fair. In preparation for the spring auction, I donated a collection of beautiful resin Santa figures hand-painted by my mom that earned me a stern lecture on how "Christmas is Jesus's birthday, not Santa's." After a sex ed lesson sent one girl careening into my office, I let her use my phone to call her parents and explain that the antiabortion video in class was too much; she wanted to go home. "I'm so sorry," I told her as she sat sniffling in my chair. As much as I wanted to, I couldn't tell her that those videos were propaganda to make girls feel ashamed of themselves and scared of sex. I couldn't tell her that within these walls, she wasn't getting the information required to make important decisions about her future. Instead, I gave hugs and dried tears while the teachers got their mail and looked us up and down, curious but not enough to reach out.

There was also the fact that I was visibly unmarried and childless. As teachers celebrated their eighteen-, nineteen-, and twenty-year-old children's weddings, I remained focused on establishing myself professionally, mostly through the graduate classes I was taking in the evenings.

"What's your master's in?" the teacher who had ixnayed my blouse on my first day wanted to know.

"English," I said. "I want to teach at a community college. When I'm finished I can hopefully pick up a few classes, see if it's really what I want."

She braced herself against the pantry counter. "Just keep in mind that what you want may not be what *God* wants for you. It's up to Him, isn't it?"

"Yes it is," I agreed, looking up from my microwaved ravioli. "The next time you talk to Him, maybe you could ask what I should do. It would save me some time."

There was one thing I couldn't reveal or push back on. A large part of navigating being queer is security, and I was operating in a place that could have dismissed me at any moment. But I was fortunate enough to finally be internally secure in who I was. I could claim the word *bisexual* and find support and validation among others like me. I could catch sight of a child's drawing of two partnered men and two partnered women holding hands under aggressive red "NO" symbols and sit sobbing in my car before pulling out of the parking lot and reminding myself of two things: that if children can be taught to hate, they can be taught not to, and that my situation was temporary. If God truly did have a plan for me, this couldn't be it.

In my last year with the school, the administration partnered with a broader network of Christian institutions that aimed to install a "biblical worldview" in their students. This organization's central tenets echoed those at our school—an emphasis on being "born again," a deep distrust of public education, and an understanding of same-sex attraction as an abomination. As this relationship intensified, staff were asked to complete a test comprised of Likert scale questions to measure the strength of their biblical worldview. The test design made it clear which answers were "correct" and which answers would brand me a Godless Pinko Commie.

Behind the mailroom partition, I filled in the bubbles according to my own convictions about morality, compassion, social justice, and respect. My responses wouldn't earn me any popularity points, but along with the unsigned policies manual at the bottom of a drawer, they were one of the gentle ways I could hold onto myself in an unaccepting space. And truthfully, these answers were no more indicative of a double life than the confessions of moms who shared that they secretly took their children trick-or-treating even though it was frowned upon. Or the volunteer who pulled me aside after a luncheon to say that she didn't think that the earth was as young as Creationism insisted. Or the grieving secretary who stood in my office doorway, closed her eyes, and whispered, "Sometimes I don't want to hear another verse of scripture. I don't want to be told to hand it over to God. I just want someone to be human with me." When you're told over and over that there is only one right way to be a righteous person, secrets swirl in the water like sediment. People commune in the whispers behind doors, the breaks in the narratives.

At this school everything about me was wrong. But I wouldn't be here forever. I would be me forever, and that was much more important.

One Sunday, I visited the local Unitarian Universalist church. It was a precarious visit, being right down the street from my workplace. Even closer was the evangelical megachurch that most of our school's families attended, featuring the massive auditorium where I had set up for the school's spring talent show. There was a good chance that someone could see me, but filling out my authentic answers to the "worldview test" had felt good. So I kept following my truth.

The Unitarian Universalist church was a repurposed old house accented by a pergola woven with flowers. Its marquee featured a flaming chalice—a symbol of love and light—and advertised when the outdoor labyrinth would be open to members and guests. The sanctuary was located around back in a separate white cottage.

I signed a guest book and maneuvered over to an empty chair where an interfaith hymnal rested. No pyrotechnics or vaulted ceilings here, no teenage boys on wailing guitars. Just an old projector screen on the back wall and a minister softly surveying everyone as they wrapped up their conversations and sat down. The music started, and someone else quickly sat down in one of the chairs to the side of the altar: a trans woman. Up until now, in and around my hometown, I had only ever seen transgender folks at the log cabin gay bar. They were usually older and kept to themselves unless approached first, with the exception of complimenting me a few times on my outfits. This woman was probably not much older than me, and I struggled not to stare at her because she was so beautiful. Her hair fell just below her chin in tight curls, and the eyeshadow she wore coordinated perfectly with her lavender, bell-sleeved dress. She didn't take her eyes off the minister. When she turned to move the purse hanging on the back of her chair, I saw the other side of her face. The burns.

It was certainly none of my business how she got these burns. She could have been a first responder. *Please be a first responder,* I thought. But I also knew that there were people out there who wanted to hurt people like us. A few weeks after we had graduated from high school, my best friend was driving around and listening to music when a van pulled up to him at a stoplight. A man stuck his head out the window to scream that *all faggots belong in hell, all faggots should die!* before slamming on the gas and tailgating him all the way to the interstate. After aggressively being run off the road multiple times, my best friend fell in line behind a police officer and the van dropped out of view. His chest was still heaving when I got to his house.

There are people who want to run us off the road, burn us, shoot us. There are others who don't want to hurt us but wish they could close their eyes and in a flash we'd cease to exist. Some of these people call themselves Christians.

Out the sanctuary window, I saw the crowds filtering out of the megachurch's doors. The trans woman picked up her hymnal and began to sing.

After the service ended I took a drive through the surrounding farmland, past the "Jesus is coming!" mailbox sign and the mobile home park with smatterings of sheds adorned with rustic country stars. I parked in a field and watched a flock of birds take off and land, like synchronized swimmers, against the watercolor mountains. David Allan Coe wailed on the radio. It was hard to get much else other than country music around here.

I smiled, remembering the time David Allan Coe wrote a scathing song about Moral Majority–darling Anita Bryant, the woman who was pied in the face by a gay man for her anti-LGBTQ "activism." In Coe's eyes, Anita Bryant was a hypocrite who should have minded her own business. Maybe, if I pressed some of my colleagues, I would find that they privately didn't have a problem with queer or transgender people. But given the child's drawing I saw that espoused learned hatred, it was safe to assume that enough of them did. Enough of them to maintain an institution that would have, according to their policies, fired me for that disclosure.

"Who are you to judge your neighbor?" James 4:12 asks. Now there was a verse for the handbook.

The next week, I turned in my resignation. Our business manager looked up at me and then down at my letter again, frantically rereading.

"It's time for me to move on," I said.

"How do I look?" I ask my best friend as I traipse out of the bathroom. He blushes and shakes his head like always, but he loves the ritual. We once spent close to an

hour pulling my limbs in and out of a knockoff Lady Gaga outfit for Halloween, fumbling like two teenagers in a closet and laugh-crying into each other's chests. Tonight is the annual underwear contest, which I enter because I can. I'll later win runner-up and share my free bar tab with the girl I've been crushing on for the past several weeks.

"So cute," he says. "There's no way she won't notice you."

I step into the night, José Esteban Muñoz's words from Disidentifications *pulsing in my heart:*

> Queerness is not yet here. Queerness is an ideality. Put another way, we are not yet queer, but we can feel it as the warm illumination of a horizon imbued with potentiality. We have never been queer, yet queerness exists for us as an ideality that can be distilled from the past and used to imagine a future. The future is queerness's domain.

The immediate future holds answers to how well I subscribe to an evangelical Christian worldview, released for the entire school to see. But in the distant future, I'll move east toward DC and Baltimore and hold hands with female partners, kiss them under umbrellas or goodbye on the train without the pressing worry of harassment. I'll earn a second graduate degree and make some new queer and trans friends in my classes. I'll meet my eventual spouse, who honors and respects my sexual orientation. I'll teach at a college where I'll never have to worry about being fired for who I am. There I will join a network for LGBTQ staff and their allies, march with this group publicly in the city Pride parade, and drape a Pride flag over my bookshelf in the hope that LGBTQ students will feel welcome and supported. They tell me that they do.

A better future. A future of our design.

Part Three

CREATIVITY, PERFORMANCE, AND EXPRESSION

A Creative Act of Faith

Joe Tolbert Jr.

I realized that it was one thing to confess your truth, but it was another thing to live it. I sat there. Tears streamed down my face as I stared at Facebook on my computer screen. I didn't know how to come to terms with the fact that God had placed something special within me but that the community that nurtured me didn't welcome me as I was created. I put the cursor in the box, with tears still streaming down my face, and I started typing. "I will be deleting Facebook for a while because a church member at my home church asked my mom how I can be a queer person and preach. Well, I'm tired of you all. I have had to fight you mean church people, and I'm going to love you from a distance cause you all are toxic to my spirit and I've fought too hard to accept the call God has on my life to go back to running and self-hate. God is love, and I will love you from a distance." I closed my laptop. I rolled myself into a ball and cried myself to sleep.

In Knoxville, Tennessee, traditions rule everything. As a kid, I was always at church. Wilder Baptist Church was my playground and a place that nurtured my spiritual becoming. As a child, I would chase my friends around the church, through radioactive green pews. On one particular day, enraptured by being chased, I made the mistake of running through the pulpit. A church mother yelled, "Stay out of the pulpit. Walk around next time!" It was at that moment that I began to see the pulpit as a space that not just anyone could occupy. I realized that the pulpit is a symbol of power in the community, and the person who occupies that space gets to define what is sacred. The preacher who occupies that space is a shaper of worlds, directly impacting people's lives. I would sit in awe of how they would spin tales that conjured the spirit and fortified us for the troubles of the week to come. With power comes great responsibility. The ability to affirm life or create death.

Home from Maynard Elementary School. I put my backpack down, grab a snack, and put my happy face forward. I answer my mother's questions to give her a recap of my day. The smile I give my mom is meant to cover up the heaviness that I feel inside. After I answer all of her questions, I go into my room, a small room with Michael Jordan posters adorning the walls. My room is the place that allows me the safety to encounter the truth of who I am becoming. In my room, I no longer have to wear the smile to cover up the struggle I have with the God I have been taught to believe. I grab my CD case, grab Yolanda Adams, and close my eyes, struggling to believe that the battle that rages inside me will one day end. I praise. I grab the Hezekiah Walker CD, advancing the tracks until I get to the track "Second Chance." "Show me all of my wrongs." My being is wrong, I think as shame envelops me. "Forgive me, and make me strong." As I sing the words to this song, my spirit is in a battle with a God that hates people who love like I love. I am pleading in spirit to have a second chance. I want to love differently. I plead. I want God to make me different. I praise. Fred Hammond's tenor fills my room, reminding me that all things are working together for my good. I praise, struggling to believe God loves me. I plead. Take this away from me. Take this away. I sing those songs until I lose myself in encountering God on my own terms, struggling to affirm what the world despises. I praise with tears flowing down my face, cleansing away the feelings of self-hate, renewing my spirit. I praise. Tears flow down my face, anointing me, wholly holy. This becomes my ritual in the secret of my room. Searching for a heaven somewhere.

Shame was a way of life for me. Never feeling good enough. Always striving to be different. Always apologizing. I am sorry for being queer. I am sorry for loving other men romantically. I am sorry for being me. Shame. What is shame other than many tiny deaths of the spirit? I lived a life apologizing, and when you live your life apologizing, you keep hidden the things God has placed within you because you don't think the treasures within are worthy of being shared. With our use of the Bible we can either affirm life or create death. My friends constantly asked how I could stay in a religious practice that denied who I was at my core. How could I love a God whose plan for me was damnation and disease? They told me that I should just leave and live life on my own terms, free of the sources of theological violence that made me hate who I was becoming, but they didn't know what happened in the secret of my childhood room. I was being transformed. My mind was being renewed amid the death masquerading as the word of the Lord. I was learning to put my faith in action, though so much still remained unknown. Though shame would continue to follow me, a foundation was laid that I would later stand on, certain of who God was to me.

I am working at an artist retreat in the mountains of Harlan County, Kentucky. I am in a session learning from Indigenous elders what it means for them to be Native women in Kentucky. As I am working the slides for the elders, I see anxious eyes appear in the glass part of the door. A crack appears, and I see half the face of my friend and a hand that is pointing at me, urgently beckoning me to come. My spirit is uneasy as we traverse the large field to get to the chapel. Some people show up unannounced to our private event and start kicking our community members out of the chapel. As I arrive at the chapel, my breathing is shallow, anxious as more people arrive on ATVs and in pickup trucks to join the disruptors, to ensure that we know we don't belong here. Life is hard, and in this political moment, I recognize the need for spaces of belonging and rest.

As the artists gather the last of their things, they try to reassure these people that everything we do is rooted in peace and love. They reply, "We ain't with that peace and love shit. We're about Jesus!" I know I have to do something. Though fear is coursing through my body with each step toward the chapel, I walk up the steps to the entrance. I see a woman leaning on the left side of the doorframe with her arms folded as if to say, "Try and get past me." I share that if we can just talk, we can move past this misunderstanding. She says nothing in response as she leans on the doorframe, blocking my entrance into the chapel. I try to enter the chapel, and she stares at me, resolute in her resistance. Realizing that they are not going to let me in and that they have no interest in talking to me, I know I have to say something to the people who are looking to me for guidance. My breathing is somewhere between fear and anxiousness. Trying to steady my breathing, I look out into their faces, scanning the crowd. While looking at them, I am trying to find the words to meet the moment of white supremacist Christianity, to meet my anger, to meet the sadness and the grief people are feeling. All I can do is trust that God has called me for moments like this. All I can do is trust that the words will be there, so I open my mouth to speak.

I didn't recognize the God of their understanding. A God that would create an us and a them. A God that would choose to expel community members from their midst instead of creating a place of radical welcome and care. It was a strange thing to manage my anger at the hate being put into the mouth of God while knowing people were looking to me for direction in a moment of white supremacist Christianity. There was no time to concern myself with the restrictions of orthodoxy, if queer people could preach or not. As I looked out into the sea of faces, they needed a word to know that God is love and that hate wouldn't have the final say. As Elandria shared with us before they became an ancestor, "It's embodiment time." It was time for me to embody my theology and take the creative act of faith to believe that my Black queer body is worthy of being a vessel for the gospel of love and liberation. When it was all said and done, my community called it a sermon. It reminded me of the role our community plays in bringing out the treasures that have been put within us. To affirm what the world despises.

I arrive at the New School to support my colleagues who are on a panel about faith and Ferguson that looks at my generation's frustrations with how our church leaders condemned protesters who showed the world that we have had enough loss of Black life at the hands of police and to demand the country see our worth every time we chant "Black Lives Matter," that Mike Brown's life mattered. The panel goes as expected. My friends and colleagues share about recovering the revolutionary politics of Jesus's ministry that was recorded in the gospels. The final speaker wraps up, and the moderator opens the floor to questions, and if you have been to enough panels, this is when the discussion elevates or you stare at your phone as people perform an intelligence that seems to suggest that they wish they were on the panel. I shift in my seat, readying myself for either way the pendulum would swing. As the last person in the line got up to the mic and began speaking, I had to put my phone down because I could feel the longing in their spirit. I look up from my phone, and I see a gender-nonconforming sibling sharing how they have wanted to maintain their relationship with God through participating in the life of a church but that they aren't always made to feel welcome. They express that they just stay at home.

As I listen, I can feel all the things they did not say. I could feel in their words the toll that living life as a queer person of faith takes on your spirit when you cannot find spiritual spaces of renewal. The panel, the majority of which are cisgender heterosexual Black men, responds with suggestions telling them to claim their space in these churches and make the congregation live out the true meaning of their faith. Something within me changes, and frustration stiffened my body as my mind recounts all the ways their advice could lead to harm. It was shocking how their concern did not take into account their safety, spiritually and physically. Shortly after, the moderator ends the question-and-answer period and thanks us for coming. My friends and I rush to them and share how they should never stay in places that make them feel they need to be anything other than who God created them to be. Before we part, we share recommendations of churches that affirm the inherent humanity and dignity of lesbian, gay, bisexual, and transgender people. We say our goodbyes, and a friend and I start walking to the train to head back uptown.

As we are walking, we hear footsteps quickly approaching. Our new friend asks, "Can I walk with you all?" "Of course," we tell them. As we walk, they begin to say those things I felt they weren't saying earlier during the Q&A. "When I came out to my parents, they kicked me out of the house. My friend who is a student at the New School has been letting me stay with him." We slow down and walk at a pace that allows us to be present for the story they are telling us. They continue, "I don't know what I am going to do, because they told me I had to leave, because I am not a student. I really don't have any place to go." It is hard bearing witness to their story knowing that there is nothing that I can do to change their situation but listen. I continue to listen, praying that in some small way our being there, listening to their story, can give the care the church refused them. We stop at the point where our journeys diverge. We say our goodbyes and continue to the train heading uptown.

I could not shake their story. Their story found a place deep in my heart. My thoughts raced. Are they safe? Do they have what they need? It pained my heart to know there was a possibility that they were roaming the streets of NYC alone. It crushed me that there wasn't much I could do to improve their situation other than providing some churches that would welcome them no matter their gender presentation. I was moved by their story because I had firsthand experiences with my community of faith acting in ways that were no different from the way people treated queer people out in the world. Many queer people have experienced harm from the church acting as if it is a private club that asks for conformity in thought and action, and if you don't share their perspectives, there is no space for you there. I could not shake their story because my queerness caused others to question my calling to ministry, enacting the same violence. In the gospels, the church is described as one body having many members, with each part of the body having its part to play and each one being valuable to the functioning of the whole. You wouldn't cut off the hand and not accept that the body would be forever changed, but far too many churches sever the queer people from their midst, and at what cost? What reflections of the divine do we miss when we sever parts of ourselves and act as gatekeepers? How would our world be different if we saw each person as a valuable part of the whole, worthy of sanctuary and care in a world that sees the least of these as disposable?

It is a beautiful spring day in Harlem, and I am walking through Marcus Garvey Park with that post-haircut pep in my step. My phone rings, and it is my mother. I take a deep breath, silently praying that this time won't be like the last time. I answer the phone and say, "Hey. How you doing?" She replies, "I am doing fine. How are you?" "I am walking back to my apartment from the barbershop," I tell her. She pauses. The silence was like she was searching for a way to say something she has kept unsaid for too long. I pray in the silence that God wouldn't let this be like the conversations we have had before. I am holding on by a thread, and I don't know how much more I can take. She puts her fear in the mouth of God and tells me, "God told me to tell you that if you don't change your ways, you are going to die of AIDS." A flood of emotion rushes over me. I am caught between shock and hurt that she would say something like this to me. A strength rose up within me, and I have had enough. I think back to the words of my queer ancestor James Baldwin:

"If the concept of God has any validity or any use, it can only be to make us larger, freer, and more loving. If God cannot do this, then it's time we got rid of him."

That does not sound like the voice of God to me. This God my mother is talking to did not make me feel larger or freer. When I stand before that God, I shrink under the weight of judgment and shame. When I stand before that God, I don't feel free. I am in bondage to the prejudices and fears people put into the mouth of God. It is time I got rid of this God. After I come back into my body, I summon the courage to speak my truth. I tell her, "That doesn't sound like the voice of God to me. How can you say that God is love in one breath and then say God told you to tell me that? I refuse to believe God is a God of hate and damnation because of who I love. If you think that is true, then that is on you." I hang up the phone feeling proud that I stood in the power of my God who is the essence of love. My God who loves me the way (s)he created me to be, and anything that asks me to be something other than that is not of God.

I walk into the chapel and sit in the heaviness of the fact that Prince is no longer with us in physical form. My classmate Melvin walks to the center of the room and waits. Prince's song "Free" begins to play, and Melvin begins to dance. I am lost in Prince's voice and Melvin's spins and sways when I realize the lyrics hit me differently this time. The chorus comes in. "Be glad that you are free. Free to change your mind." I didn't feel free. The certainty with which most Christians approach God made me feel imprisoned to traditions and other people's revelations. I keep returning to the question "Have I given my power away? My freedom?" The revelations of who I know God to be are my own, revealed to me through my Black queer life, but those revelations are the very things putting me at odds with my family, my community. The certainty that most Christians approach an unknowable God just ends up remaking God in the image of their prejudices. I know I am approaching a crossroads. I can keep things the way they are or find the freedom to reimagine God through my journey of becoming the queer me I know myself to be. After the dance, people stand at the podium reflecting on what Prince means to them. I think back to when I was a kid and the first time I watched *Purple Rain* with my family on TV and how there was a sensuality that drew me to him. I think back to the ways in which Prince gave me the permission to be the queer child I was becoming. I think about the unbridled freedom that he invites us into and how the personal freedom within demands that we re-create that freedom in the world. I think about the time my mother surprised my sister and me with tickets to his show and the emotion I felt seeing him sing about the purple rain. I come back to myself as the last person takes their seat.

A hush falls on the chapel. Then over the speakers we hear that first strum of the opening chord to "Purple Rain." As I sit there, I hear Prince sing about not meaning to cause any sorrow or pain. I think of my mother and the journey we are on. In my rational mind, I know the hurt I am experiencing is not intentional, but what her God demands in matters of love and the question of my soul is eternal, so isn't it an expression of love to not want your child to burn in hell forever? It is something in this song that allowed me the space to admit to myself that I am hurting from her words that pierce my spirit. I am hurting not just for me but for all the Black queer people of faith who encounter other people's God that is birthed from a limited theological imagination and leads to the outcome of queer antagonism and theologies of damnation and disease. I hurt for the Black queer person who didn't find open arms but bullying from kids spewing hate they learn from their parents, leading queer youth to suicide. I wish they could dance in the purple rain, that loving, cleansing rain. Now I hear the beginning of that moving guitar solo, and what were silent tears at the beginning of the song are now a flood. I cannot help thinking of the young person I met at the New School and wish them love, joy, and community. I don't realize the song has long since ended because I am overcome by the tears coming down from someplace deep within. I feel arms embrace me. I feel bodies surrounding me. I try to open my eyes, but I cannot see clearly. I make out a blurry Dean Wilson as the person whose embrace engulfs me. She asks, "What's wrong?" I try to form words to form sentences, but it comes out in a jumble: "Young . . . adult . . . homeless . . . because . . . queer . . . my mom . . . me . . . hell . . . I'm queer." Each attempt at a sentence is punctuated by deep inhales of air and sniffs from my nose. A hand from the crowd around me hands me some tissue. Dean Wilson begins to pray, and soon a chorus of voices join in. They create beautiful music through the sound of my tears. Their faith fills the gap my doubt leaves between the current world I experience and the loving world I want to live in. Their prayers strengthen my spirit as I continue to stand, having nothing left to do. As everyone around me says amen, I come back to myself, a little lighter, more determined to endure my mother's religious homophobia. Dean Wilson grabs my shoulders and looks me in the eye and says, "You love people. Have you ever considered that those are the people God is calling you to serve?"

It is one thing to confess my truth, but it is another thing to live it. I spent so much time fighting theologies of hate that I didn't have time to build anything that could help shield the spirits of people who were going through similar things as I was. Tradition is a complicated thing. The Black church tradition has so many beautiful things about it, and my love for it is what keeps me seeking ways to carve out a place for queer existence in the tradition that raised me and, oddly enough, feeds my spirit. Tradition can also trap the living God into the ways things were done in the past and lead us to a blind acceptance without asking why and who these traditions actually serve. To live my truth, I've had to confront the fear of breaking with what I was taught to be true and lean into the truth of God that is still unfolding for me.

I had to take a creative act of faith and break with tradition and trust the new path my relationship with God is taking me on. It is a creative act of faith to believe that God loves my Black queer self. A creative act of faith that affirms that I too am called to share the gospel of the good news of a God that loves all of us and all the ways we love. A creative act that knows God is love and that God is (self)Love, and that this love of God and myself necessitates a reimagining of the traditions so that we can manifest more love for those who have been made to feel like outcasts before God. To live in this creative act of faith has required me to join with others and continue in the tradition of those Black queer Christians before me who have made the road by walking us into a new vision of God and community that has no need for homophobia that is said to be the voice of God. A new vision of God and community that says the body of Christ is made better when we celebrate the humanity and divinity of all of God's creation as integral to the work of the church as an embodiment of *on earth as it is in heaven*, making that vision real.

Role Play

JARRED JOHNSON

For three nights when I was fifteen, I played a school shooter. My church put the play on every few years: *Heaven's Gates & Hell's Flames*. The mission was to evangelize new Christians. My mother thought it was important I watch it. She wanted to mold my reality to hers, but as a child, I cried watching it and made her take me out of the auditorium. Occasionally demons slinked through the aisles and startled you. During a scene in which two teenage girls overdosed on heroin, strobe lights flashed across the stage before Satan emerged through fabric flames, his face scarred and painted red, to carry the girls off to hell.

To exorcise my childish fears, I joined the performance as a teen. I thought becoming the scary thing could make me unafraid. Behind the scenes, I saw my fears disassembled—the costumes, makeup, lights, and sounds. Each night I carried a backpack onstage with a prop gun inside it. I stood in front of my locker. After two bullies taunted me and my coach kicked me off the football team and the girl I had a crush on denied me, I reached for the gun and started shooting, then I put it under my chin, and when I heard a loud pop through the speakers, I threw my head back and fell to the ground.

Satan came onstage with horns and a pitchfork. "Josh," he said. A vocal effect in his microphone echoed each word an octave lower, so when he grunted or laughed, it deepened and repeated. "You did good, boy. They all deserved to die, and now you get to spend eternity in hell with me."

It was 2008. *Batman: The Dark Knight* was in theaters. Though there weren't many things in the news cycle that I yet paid attention to, I knew Heath Ledger died of an overdose while playing the Joker. He was a *Method Actor*, someone who went to great lengths to align his physical, emotional, and psychological selves with his characters. I understood it was possible for a performance to bleed over into an actor's life—character fueling identity, identity fueling character.

I thought of Heath Ledger when I got cast as Josh. The role wasn't serious enough, nor was I a good enough actor to confuse myself with a school shooter, but I tried to summon some of Josh's feelings. When I stepped out from behind the curtain, I wasn't Jarred; I was him. The girl I liked hurt me. My coach kicked me off the team. The boys at school bullied me. That part I understood. I was bullied at school for being gay, though that wasn't yet an identity I accepted, not yet a role that felt authentic to play.

Each night after *Heaven's Gates* was over, I stood at the altar with the rest of the actors. The pastor took the stage behind us. "If anyone wants to devote your life to Jesus," he said, "the people by the altar are ready to pray with you." We had been given a script for that part too: *Do you believe Jesus died on the cross for your sins? Do you ask him into your life? Do you have a home church?*

Laying my hands on the shoulders of the men who approached me, leading them in prayer, I reckoned with the power of performance. I believed then I had exposed the audience to the harsh realities of hell, but looking back on my childhood fears, I also knew art could be a tool of manipulation. The culture we consume shapes our identities, feelings, and beliefs. Performance, as much as it creates the act and the actor, creates the viewer too.

Before I was old enough to see them, I watched the movies my father loved—Westerns mostly, war movies, action films. We sat together at the TV after dinner, past our windows the Appalachian foothills of southern Kentucky. I was six, ten, twelve. It was *Tombstone*, *Saving Private Ryan*, *Die Hard*. It was *Butch Cassidy and the Sundance Kid*, *Cold Mountain*, and *Dances with Wolves*. These films were my earliest education in masculinity, belief, Americanness, performance—all of them knotted tightly together. Because the films showed things my young eyes shouldn't see, Dad invented a word: *fakey*.

"Turn that off," Mom would say when his films showed violence. Sometimes I hid my eyes in her shoulder.

"Aw, Annie," Dad would answer, a flick of his wrist to dismiss her. "That's just fakey."

The diminutive *EY* suffix rendered his word cute, palatable, harmless—like the concept itself. It's just Hollywood, *fakey* implied: illusion, an act, all artifice. The cowboy riddled with bullets: fakey. The soldier who lost an arm in an explosion: fakey. The gaping wounds, the peeled back flesh: all fakey.

But even as I was reminded everything was fake, I knew the power of movies to make me feel. This is *suspension of disbelief*: acceptance of unreality in favor of following an emotional response. More than to appease Mom's critiques, I think Dad invented *fakey* to comfort me. He watched his movies trouble me. He saw me happy, anxious, scared, excited. I cared about what Dad cared about, rooted for the characters he rooted for.

Dad never cried during movies, but Mom did: when the Sioux warrior Wind in His Hair yelled "I am your friend" from the hilltop in *Dances with Wolves*, when Captain Miller said, "James, earn this" in *Saving Private Ryan*. For years I wrestled with Dad's stoicism, his absence. I determined, like Mom, to feel; I cried at his movies.

Developed by Russian theater practitioner Konstantin Stanislavski, the technique known as *Method Acting* guides an actor past imitating characters and toward embodying them, substituting the actor's feelings, motivations, and desires for those of the character. Onstage, the distinction between actor and character ceases to exist; instead, the two merge into what Stanislavski called a "third being," *artisto-rol* in Russian, an amalgamated persona that combines the actor's personality and experience with the character's. Stanislavski spoke of "living the part." He wanted the actor to become "completely carried away by the play . . . not noticing how he feels, not thinking about what he does." Importantly, even when diverging from the script, when improvising, for example, the actor behaves as the character.

Stanislavski used what he called "sense memory" to unite the actor with the role. Recalling formative emotional experiences from their own life, the actor allows those real experiences to connect with the emotional landscape of their character. More than just an outward representational performance, sense memory unites the psychological terrains of both actor and character; the actor doesn't just cry to represent the character's emotions but pulls from their own history to truly feel what the character feels. Stanislavski also believed in the superiority of the body to achieve his desired substitution. Through bodily action, including his ideas of animal work, studying animal movement to capture a character's physicality, Stanislavski believed the actor's unconscious could be summoned, thus integrating the actor and character more deeply than through emotional, conscious tethering.

In college my friends and I often drove the hour south from Bowling Green, Kentucky, to the gay club Play Nashville. It was a playground where I could express other sides of myself, trying on identities to see if they fit. Past the entrance line and through the club's doors, the tops of both my hands marked with black Xs, I traveled inside myself somewhere new. In the world I was from, I was taught to rein in my desiring eyes that longed to linger on the succulent, rippling parts of a man: his thick arms and wide back, the blade of his jaw, the peekaboo of skin above his waistline as he stretched.

In the architecture of that club, drag was the portal I passed through to self-acceptance. In the room where you entered, small cocktail tables and chairs surrounded a large stage with an extended runway. It was where the drag queens performed before the dance floor opened. Miss Deception, Vanity, Nichole Ellington Dupree, all the queens lip-synced to music I loved—Dolly Parton, Beyoncé, Ariana Grande, The Chicks—kicking, jumping, spinning, and splitting.

To tip them, I stood at the edge of the stage with a dollar bill raised. Sometimes while taking the tips from me, the queens leaned their heads down, offering their cheeks for a kiss. It felt like worship, the way the music dipped then swelled, the queens' bodies enlivening the sounds. In the audience we stood rapt, our attention focused together, communing as one.

When the dance floor opened, my friends and I moved there. Around me boys danced with boys, girls with girls. Men touched men with the longing handholds of attraction. I danced freely there, claiming an autonomy I had seen modeled first by the drag queens. In that space femme was nothing to fear. I threw my head back and lifted my hands, I twisted my hips, and I let my eyes roam in a way I had always guarded. My first kiss with a guy was on that dance floor. He had bangs spiked with gel and rhinestoned fleurs-de-lis on his butt pockets. We brushed against one another as we danced, but both of us held tight, charged by the connection. Soon he reached for my face and brought his to meet mine.

Until I was eight, my family went to a Pentecostal church called Calvary. We pulled our hymnals from beside fans with a white Jesus's face on them in the backs of the pews. My sister and mom reached for their tambourines. The preacher's wife, hair teased tall, face pale, sat her tiny frame behind the piano to play. Sometimes Brother Ernie called me to the front to sing. I was known for "Enemy's Camp."

"Well I went to the enemy's camp," I sang, "took back what he stole from me. Now he's under my feet, under my feet. Satan is under my feet."

Years later at a very different kind of church—a nondenominational one where the pastor spoke from a stage through a headset mic, a video of him broadcast on screens to his left and right—I started leading worship. I performed holiness, hitting the notes, moving my hands like I was supposed to, closing my eyes, saying the right words. But I always had doubts I was discouraged from exploring or expressing. I never spoke in tongues, even though my pastors tried to teach me. I never heard the voice of God like others said they did. All the spiritual things, all the miracles, even the exorcisms, which I twice witnessed, always made me deeply uncomfortable. Praying for other people, approaching strangers to talk about God, even the fundamental call to convert someone to believe what I was taught never felt right to me.

Since I had grown up performing, I was keenly aware when I stepped into a role. I recognized faith as a performance too. Rituals made it stronger, repeated acts. You went to church, you prayed, you read your Bible. The role of a Christian necessitated certain ways of speaking, dressing, acting. It carried requirements of gender and sexuality. The strong husband was holy, as was the modest wife. I saw the role I needed to inhabit, but I couldn't live the part.

Masculinity was a role I didn't accept and a role that didn't accept me. Its demands were strict and clear in southern Kentucky. Hunting and fishing, sports and video games were masculine. Sex was masculine, objectification. Stoicism was masculine—rigidity, swagger.

I was called *Gay* before I claimed the identity for myself. The boys at school saw it in me: my twisting hips, expressive hands, how I formed my lips to speak. To them I was Gay, Sissy, Faggot. I was Limp Wrist, Flamer, Homo. I batted for the other team. My parents saw I was gay too. My mother was a careful arbiter of queerness. At every glance, she called it out as though, like the word *Jesus*, the power of expulsion were in its name. She once caught me in my sister's bedroom walking in her beauty pageant heels. I stood silent and shaking when she opened the door. Usually delicate and poised, Mom hardened. She ripped the shoes from my feet and bent me over the footboard to spank me. To my mother, crossing a gendered boundary was to deny God and nature.

Boyish was a happy identity to me—I was curious, playful, energetic—but when masculinity was imposed on my growing body, I felt squeamish and uncomfortable. My dad defined himself primarily by work, so he was absent—often physically, completely emotionally. Careful with cleanliness, Dad stripped to his underwear in the laundry room as soon as he got home from work. He walked to his shower, tired feet shuffling, shoulders slouched, farmer's tan. Whatever energy he expelled at the mattress store he owned left nothing for me. I defined myself as his antonym, crafting an identity around what he was not. He liked work, the outdoors, and basketball, so I liked books, music, theater, and the internet.

Like the performance of faith, gender's performance rests too on manipulation. In this case, the actor seeks to manipulate themselves. Like Stanislavski's *sense memory*, the performance tethers the mental and emotional landscapes of actor and character so tightly the two are indistinguishable. The actor wants to rest certain the performance is legitimate; gender is inherent, stable—not a performance at all.

❧

Inhabiting the role of a worship leader necessitates acting. The swell of ambient chords, the riff of a guitar, the steady rhythm of the drums, my voice even, my prayers, created real, emotional responses from people. From the stage, I watched the audience and lost myself in the performance. They sang and shouted, wept and danced. Sometimes people fell to their knees or pressed their faces to the ground, prostrate before God, awed by his holiness. It was the intoxicating feeling I longed for as a believer. I was taught a worship leader was the vessel through which God's presence reached earth. I could almost picture it: the Holy Spirit moving past my doubts and sins to emerge through me.

Once during a revival, I was onstage playing the keyboard. A visiting pastor turned to me behind him just before the altar call. I remember his words clearly: "Can you pray the house down?" I knew what he wanted. I was a senior in high school then, just about to move away to college, desperately wanting to embrace that I was gay. The pastor wanted a loud, passionate oration, something emotional to draw people to the altar to give their lives to God, but I couldn't summon it; I couldn't persuade people to do something I didn't feel.

I prayed in the microphone that day, but looking out over the audience, I recognized my complicity. I wondered if there were other queer people in the crowd. Maybe my worship or prayers told them to repent from their wicked ways, to deny their desires, to value God and his supposed wishes over the desires their bodies, like mine, instinctually possessed.

I call my drag persona *Coal, the Appalachian Queen*. She performs regularly at a gay-owned restaurant in Wilmington, North Carolina, where I now live. She's been a part of my life since college. Coal retains the best parts of me but shrugs off what doesn't serve her. Unlike in my waking life, Coal is liberated from the strictures of Jarred's past. I feel that when I take to the stage; I'm carried away by the play. Like the crowd cheering in the darkness beyond the bright lights, everything behind me recedes.

At some point in each transformation into drag, you become almost unrecognizable to yourself. Cheekbones emerge where seemingly none existed. Your forehead lowers, nose thins. Your eyes grow and change shape, and you start to feel, staring at what had just been your reflection, someone else looking back at you. For me, my facial expressions change, as do my posture and my voice. It's a kind of possession, an inhabitation, the seamless merging of actor and character, Stanislavski's *third person*.

Sometimes when I'm getting in drag, I see my mother. Her femininity is overexaggerated. A traditional Southern woman, she curls her hair and teases it high. She won't let anyone see her without a full face of makeup. She always wears jewelry and perfume. Despite being tall and learning at a young age to slouch to minimize herself, Mom carries herself with a careful grace I sought to replicate. Her hips make rhythm as she moves. Her fingers speak. When she talks on the phone, her lips move to match the speaker's on the other line. When I'm getting in drag, I watch myself in the mirror. In the right light, at the right angle, I see my mother, smiling.

When I came out to my parents as gay at twenty, my mom's first suggestion was for me to drop out of college. She wanted to send me to a school for worship in Redding, California. She thought it would save me. Draw closer to God, she believed, devote your life to worshiping him, and you will see the truth.

"There's a song in you that no one else can sing," she texted me recently. That's typical language for her. "I pray it will bubble up from your heart today."

Music is important to my mom and to her understanding of me. It's something she often says. From upstairs at our house, she listened to me playing piano, writing worship songs in her basement. There were years of my life when I thought music was important to me too. I thought I would write and record songs and continue leading worship. My mom's favorite artists were mine.

When I think of the moment my mom was most proud of me, I think of the Sunday at church when I sang the worship song I wrote, when her vision of me was the same one I was performing.

The mountain lifts up its face, I wrote.
The ocean bows to your name
The earth and sky exist to bring you fame
And who am I that you would care to know my name?
Who am I to not see all your glory?
Who am I to not believe you go before me?

I struggle to understand if I believed those words when I wrote them or if I was performing belief the way I felt I had to.

In his essay "Girl," Alexander Chee describes drag as "a theater of being female more than a reality . . . costumes, an illusion, a spell you can cast on others and yourself." Performance is the defining difference, the awareness of that performance. To be a woman means to feel embodied as a woman. To do drag is to exaggerate the performance of a woman. The hair is bigger, waist smaller, hips rounder, makeup thicker. Drag is a parody of womanhood that pokes holes, in fact, in the assumptions of what femininity is. Drag is illusion. The performer embodies not an identity but a character, and after the show is over that character disappears until they are summoned again through paint and foam, fabric and hair.

Drag's comfort for many viewers rests precisely in this illusion; drag is comfortable because it's not real. There is nothing threatening about performance—it is, after all, created, artifice, *fakey*. Unlike performance, identity rests on belief. Identity is a faith—a strong-held conviction that even when tested, no one can refute. I think of Hebrews 11:1, which defines *faith* this way: "assurance of things hoped for, the conviction of things not seen."

Binaries are the foundation of the Christianity I grew up in, the distinct separation of what is holy from what is secular. In one realm is our world, all our human creations, our songs and art and entertainment, all the lusts of our flesh. Then in another realm is the spiritual: heaven and hell, angels and demons, God and Satan, good and evil that are constantly in warfare, just like in *Heaven's Gates & Hell's Flames*, over each of our souls. To enter into the kingdom of God, to live eternally in heaven, is to commit yourself to a life of holiness. To be unholy is to step outside God's grace, to sin, to transgress. It means favoring the flesh and its desires over God's will.

I came out as nonbinary on a drunken night after a Pride event at a brewery in Wilmington. I drank a few beers. I talked to friends. I bought a necklace and some lace socks from queer vendors, then I went to the table of the local LGBT center. They had bowls full of plastic armbands like the yellow Livestrong ones everyone wore when I was in middle school, except these armbands listed pronouns. I wore a skirt that day. I had put on eyeshadow in a gradient of the rainbow, and I considered myself as I stared at the bowls of bracelets. In yellow was *he/him*, the pronouns I had used my entire life. Beside it, a bowl of green bracelets saying *they/them*. I picked up both sets of bracelets. A few hours later, spinning in a hammock swing on one of my friend's porches, I held up my wrists and cried. "I never let myself be this," I said, "but it's who I am."

I often present quite masculine. Like many gay men, I pursue muscles that elude me. I go the gym often. I watch my diet. In my formative years, I shunned masculine things. I see how my relationship to gender impacted my relationship to place, to home. To me the outdoors was masculine—the land, the foothills of the Appalachian mountains, my family's farm; men hunted, they fished, they plowed and bushhogged and four-wheeled. The land was a space of dominion, domination.

This understanding of nature is, of course, based on the Bible—Genesis 1:26: "Then God said, 'Let us make human beings in our image, to be like us. They will reign over the fish in the sea, the birds in the sky, the livestock, all the wild animals on the earth, and the small animals that scurry along the ground.'"

Already feeling ostracized from everything masculine, I shunned the place I was from. I spent most of my time in my room, reading, writing, trying to find a community of knowledge and belonging in the internet to replace the lack of belonging I felt where I was. *Coal, the Appalachian Queen* is one way I reclaim my relationship to home. Now I have many women's clothing items in my closet: dresses, skirts, blouses, heels. Sometimes I wear makeup, bringing some of the skills I learned in drag into my daily life, bridging performance and identity in a direct way. Comparing myself to other nonbinary people I know, I question if the term is right for me. I don't question how the pronouns *they* and *them* feel when used for me: they're cozy, liberating. With *they,* I get to define the terms on which I perform gender. I am not working within a confine that is masculinity, embracing some elements while opposing others. Less than a role, its delineations feel permeable.

The last time I tried to heal my relationship to Christianity was in 2017. I was living in Chicago then, and I went to a service at a church called Urban Village. They sold merch with their name on it and the slogan "Queerly Beloved." I recognized some of the worship leaders as queer; they had the same signifiers the boys in school saw in me: high speaking voices, expressive hands, curated clothing and presentation. I expected to be shocked by the contradictions—seeing queerness and worship, the two warring elements of my youth, held together—but nothing about it looked unnatural. At a coffee shop a few days later, the pastor spoke to me and answered my questions.

"I'm so sorry," she said, "for how the church treated you. Think of what we lost out on. Not just you and your talents but so many queer people's."

I revel now in the space of simultaneous belief and disbelief—the playground where I accept and deny, know and am unsure. I still can't watch horror movies about demon possessions. Sometimes when I'm scared I speak the name of *Jesus*, still believing in its power. I do not wish to say that my mother's beliefs or those of the people in her church are fake. Instead, I wish to say belief is buffered by performance; performance creates the actor, creates faith, creates identity.

For me I'm not sure. I've seen the ways Christianity demonizes me as a queer person and drag performer. I've felt firsthand its dehumanization, the oppressive forces of its demands, the way it ranks sins and disregards scholarship that challenges its ideas. I've seen Christians vote against humanity in too many elections to believe they care about what they claim. Faith seems like it should be life-transforming, not a set of strictures by which to abide. As a young person, I was taught to judge a Christian by their fruit, the metaphor for the actions and outlook a believer takes. The fruit seems rotten. To clean it out, I travel to the source: the vine, the base, the root. Perhaps I am tilling the garden, turning over new earth to start again.

❧

I don't often sing or play the piano anymore, though I still own the one my mother bought me. It sits in my office on the wall opposite the desk where I write, a transfiguration perhaps of my modes of expression, worship. Occasionally I still listen to worship music. The sounds and chords feel familiar. I like the passion the worship leaders bring. What they sing about often feels more authentic than many of the radio songs about love.

Though I don't go to church, I play in a queer kickball league each Sunday in Wilmington. Each season we host a lip-sync battle at the local gay club as a fundraiser for a youth services nonprofit. This past year my team and I performed to "Barbie Girl" by Aqua. All the performers got ready together upstairs. We scattered our costumes and wigs and makeup bags across a pool table. Costumed as cheerleaders, plastic dolls, and hair band rock stars, we laughed and drank, took photos and practiced our choreography. There were a few mirrors along the walls we used to get ready. Putting on my makeup in one, I summoned Coal.

Another team chose the song "Unholy" by Sam Smith and Kim Petras. For their costumes they chose nuns' habits and priestly vestments. I watched from the audience while they performed. The lights strobed red. During the chorus—*Mummy don't know daddy's getting hot at the body shop doing something unholy*—two of the priests stripped off their robes to reveal glittering Lycra underwear. It reminded me of *Heaven's Gates & Hell's Flames*, only now the imagery felt powerless—pure performance, camp, a farce.

When I think of my parents' church and worship, I think of gay clubs—nights like that lip-sync battle where a community of people like me, who had gone through similar hardships, stood together, in the South in this case, in a place that seems to want to reject us, with our eyes focused on the same stage, watching other queer people dance and twirl, and we sang along, believing in the power of community, feeling, after years of not, a sense of belonging right there where we were. That's church.

Sources:

Chee, Alexander. "Girl." *Guernica*, March 16, 2015.

Stanislavsky, Konstantin. *An Actor Prepares*. Theatre Arts, Inc., 1936.

Let Us Sing

Davis Shoulders

In the spring of 2002, my family took a vacation to Cades Cove in the Great Smoky Mountains. After a week of sightseeing, hiking, and biking "the cove," they informed me and my siblings we would be moving back to East Tennessee that summer. My dad had taken a new preaching job in Maryville, Tennessee. In some of the early conversations around the reasons for the move from Middle Tennessee was the notion that this region was a "mission field" for the churches of Christ. Middle Tennessee was chock-full of CoCs on every corner in every county. But in Blount County, one of the largest geographic counties in the region, there were only three churches that shared our name and doctrine.

I was born in Knoxville, Tennessee, in 1992 while my dad was preaching at the Karns Church of Christ. We then spent my toddler years in the hills of Southwest Virginia at a tiny country church in Martinsville. We moved away from Appalachia in order to be closer to my grandparents. But fate would bring us back to the hills of East Tennessee, where I would grow up in the "mission field." My dad was involved in the planting of two more churches in the region, one in Sevier County and one in Blount County.

My dad often used quotes from his children in his sermons to make his points stronger, whether they were factual or embarrassing to us or not. Since the name of the church my dad preached at was Eastside Church of Christ, I was quoted as saying, "We're gonna build a Northside, a Westside, and a Southside Church of Christ." Whether these were my words or my father's words I cannot recall. But the sentiment of the mission field was embedded in our family's journey in the return to my native land of East Tennessee.

❧

There are some things that are too precious to speak aloud.

Like the god of my childhood, sacred names were uttered only in a certain holy reverie. They could not be trivialized or diminished or taken in vain. Even though we have allowed god to be on our lips, even older traditions do not speak or write their respective deities' names.

When I begin to speak on a different aspect of my identity, one more physically attuned to my embodiment and performance of the self, I feel the same way.

As something that can be understood only by me.

There is a quiet whisper in my brain that calls upon my queerness. That my god-given gender means so much more than a person knowing what's between my legs.

❧

I've always loved singing hymns in church.

The songleader would announce a song, asking us to turn to a particular hymn, telling us which verses we were singing, lifting their hand aloft, readying to conduct us, as if to hold the first note in the air before we all joined in.

This ritual phrasing, calling us to sing, calling us to worship, holds an excitement for me still. I can imagine hymnal numbers being called out. The shuffling of pages. The satisfying aahs from people whose favorite song was just called. Being asked to stand for a particular song. That was the good part of the church. The part I always cared about.

I would get compliments on my singing. Not because my voice was particularly beautiful or on pitch or I sang the right notes and rhythm. I sang robustly. From somewhere deep within me.

As I grew older, the words began to feel strange across my tongue. But I quickly realized that I cared less about the words I was singing and more about the feeling evoked from the resonance of old-sounding language in folk hymns.

At many of the churches my family attended, we had old hymnals. Printed sometime in the mid-century. It was always strange to go to a church with the newest edition of the hymnal. There's something about going to a small country church in Appalachia and singing out of a hymnal where the binding is busted and worn out. Walking out of the front doors into the sunlight to see a mountain rearing its beautiful green-glazed head above you. I've been to those places. I've worshiped there. My dad preached at those churches. I was held in these spaces by the real singing that took place. Not for the beautiful harmony but for the clarity and honesty of the voices resonating through the pews and into the mountain air.

One morning I board a plane to Europe.

That same morning my grandmother enters into the joy of the Lord.

This is my first flight ever, even at the age of nineteen. I am going to Europe for three months for my study abroad program. I feel the gravity of the day as I document my expectation and excitement in my journal.

My grandmother is in the hospital. My dad and his siblings are there. We don't know how much longer she has, but the sentiment is shared with me that there's no reason to stay back in the States and miss the opportunity.

"Grannie Rose wouldn't want you to miss your flight."

I don't know Grannie Rose that well. I have memories of drinking out of glass Coke bottles and eating frozen pizzas in her small dorm-mother suite at the Christian university I will eventually attend in West Tennessee.

From then on we meet at the occasional Thanksgiving dinner or whenever we're passing through her neck of the woods. She has a stuffed dog that I learn to pet but that kinda freaks me out too. She always lives in small settings. Eventually assisted living homes where we sometimes bring dinners to host in the community room on the first floor. She has a thick mid-south accent and a slow drawl that is augmented by her age. It sometimes peaks into sharper notes when she needs you to hear her. But it's her gentle gaze and smile that I remember most. Sometimes she requests I play piano for her or that we sing for her while she closes her eyes and leans her head back to rest with a gentle knowing.

I'm driving to the airport with my mom. I call Dad to see how Grannie Rose is doing. The receiver picks up, and it is one of my aunts on the line. She whispers into the phone. "Your dad can't talk right now, but we wanted to let you know Grannie Rose just passed away."

I don't know how close the timing of my call was to her spirit leaving the body, but it feels as if I called the moment she left.

We keep driving to the airport. Not knowing yet how to process the grief of her loss and yet feeling awkward about getting on the plane. I do not tell anyone in our traveling group of twenty or so students that my grandmother just died. It's too much to explain right now.

The plane travel is exhausting. We land in Brussels with barely enough energy to carry our massive bags stuffed with three months' worth of personal belongings. Someone slowly orients us toward the train that will take us to our beds. We transfer a few lines and walk out of the train station into the streets of a small Belgian town.

A week later, we attend our first "French" church service. The Christian university I studied at has a facility above a church in Verviers, Belgium. We walk down the stairs Sunday morning, meeting the French-speaking church members.

Quickly I feel a subdued air, something larger than the language barrier. People are quiet, and not the kind of sleepy Sunday morning quiet. A deeper quiet.

Our raucous cadre of American students takes up several rows in the church. Slowly the sanctuary fills up with regular members and announcements begin to be made. We have a designated translator to help us understand what's going on in the service. But we sing in French. They are the same hymns, the same tunes, same syllables. It's easy enough to hum along and read the words on the page without knowing what you are even saying. The hymn still speaks for itself.

The songleader begins to falter on the second song following an opening prayer. You can feel his emotions getting the best of him. He can't finish the song and steps away. A few people attend to him, and you start to hear quiet sniffles around the church. The church wants to put on a good face for us, but something has clearly happened.

Our translator makes a quiet announcement to us in English explaining that one of the matriarchs of the church had passed away last night. The church is in mourning for her. She was loved by all, and the songleader, a relative of hers, just couldn't keep it together. This worship service becomes an unofficial funeral for this dearly beloved woman.

I feel something sink and unlock in my chest. Every hymn I begin to sing with a different gravitas. And tears stream down my face as I participate in the funeral for this woman and my own grandmother at the same time.

I feel my grandmother is with me in this tiny church in Belgium.

I get to say goodbye to her after all.

⁂

If you asked me if I believe in god, I would answer yes and no.

At times, god is the real entity hovering over us all. Not just the god of the Bible but the god of all religions. The force in name or in notion that represents what is beyond, what is nondual in nature. The mystery of a sense of being that knows more, sees more, and guides the events of the day to bring about the evolution of the human species toward a gentle sense of a higher path.

When I say no, I mean to reject the small gods, the limiting doctrine and theology that invite us to hurt other people at the expense of our god.

⁂

For my thirtieth birthday party, I invited people to a birthday baptism ritual.

We met out on my friend's farm in Greene County, Tennessee, at a bend in the Nolichucky River with shallow shoals. I invited everyone to wear white, and I waded out into the river in a thrifted white dress and got dunked to an echo of singing voices from the shoreline.

I was craving this renewal, this reclamation of a tradition that hadn't felt very momentous in my childhood.

I did not need to speak the name or authority under which I was baptized. I just needed people whom I loved to witness this act. This clarifying ritualistic moment. Dipping myself in a stream that flowed down from somewhere higher up in elevation.

⊰ ⊱

The Nolichucky River has healing powers. Ask folks around Upper Northeast Tennessee about dipping in the Nolichucky. You are bound to hear incredible stories.

A neighbor friend of mine once shared a sacred moment on the Nolichucky. After a less than healthy rebounding phase and seeing her ex for the first time, my friend found herself driving near the river.

A roadside peach stand appeared. She stopped. An easy embankment by the river to descend. She stopped. Scaled the bank. Stripped her clothes. Carrying a single peach with her out to the center of the river.

Her tears and the juices of the peach spilled down her body and blended in with the flow of the river. Once she was done with the first peach, she went back to the shore and grabbed another. And repeated until all her tears were cleansed in the water.

She ritualized her own healing. She let the river sing to her.

⊰ ⊱

Queerness in its own way can feel like a mission field.

You have this truth within you. That you decide to be brave enough to express. To come out. To acknowledge that your identity may not fit within the traditional notions of gender and sexuality.

We are burdened with the proof of our existence, much like Christians feel burdened by the truth of proving their god.

But I was never for door-knocking and evangelical media campaigns. I like conversations.

I like knowing that I am being seen and felt in the safety of people who desire that.

The truth of my queerness is not hidden; it simply does not share itself in undeserving spaces.

It's ineffable, like the moment of grief shared in a Belgian church with someone else's grandmother and my own. It pours out of me when it wants to. And it protects and defends its way and others around me when needed.

It is not ashamed of its own power. For its safety, though, it must be guarded. At the ready to give an answer to anyone who asks of me. And to know when the pearls are before swine who would rather kill us in the streets than acknowledge our beauty.

I don't attend church anymore. But that statement feels false in my mouth.

I attend a church of my own making. At any place where a sense of knowing is felt. At any place where a deeper resonance calls from the hills around us and begs us to look up or down or inward or outward.

I'll find myself humming or singing aloud old hymns as I carry on with my day. I'm reminded of a particular renowned preacher, songleader, and professor who would jaunt about the campus of Lipscomb University singing as he made his daily walking commutes. Always a song in your heart. It's something that I do myself. Wherever I am, when an outdated theological tune comes to mind, I sing anyway. I don't explain to those around me that I am not worshiping the god I used to with those words, but I am worshiping. I am connected to an inner spirit. The unashamed hopefulness of those tunes. My reclamation of its use in my life. A balm for the soul. The paradox of the words and the meanings still do not get in the way of the feeling these tunes evoke. They pull on my queer soul and send it out in my adoration and gratitude for the messy world we live in.

Once I attended a fundraiser for the Highlander Research and Education Center hosted in the Sequoyah Hills neighborhood in West Knoxville. I recognized a few faces from various activist events around the city. It felt much like my grad school dinner parties back in DC. The intergenerational feeling of organizers who were having a family dinner for a righteous cause. And then there was a call to sing. The sound of these old protest hymns echoed through the vaulted ceiling of the living room. It felt like church again, people asking for their favorite songs to be led. It felt like a church that matched a newfound political perspective, and yet it also pulled on the emotional and spiritual resonance of my childhood. The gathering was a fundraiser for a new archival center on the Highlander Center campus in New Market, Tennessee. Some of the same archives that were destroyed by a fire in March 2019 where a white power symbol was found on the grounds. We sing through fire.

While living in DC, my church friends and I would go out dancing Saturday night and then roll up to church the next morning to join singing practice. My body still responding to the sensual consumption of the previous night yet enjoying the cleanness and sacredness of the new morning. Still smelling of sweat and alcohol, even after a shower and a couple of McDonald's hash browns, I would look over and smirk at my friends who shared in the evening's debauchery and the hangovers like a delightful secret. Keeping it all together in an exceptional cycle of excess and discipline. Evening church and morning church were one and the same.

❧

The musicality of the church is often a saving grace for us queer folks, whether or not we had identified that part of our gender and sexuality at the time. The pageantry, the performance of religion gives people like me an outlet, desiring the aesthetics of an activity to make up for the drudgery of church doctrine. It's a necessary distraction. An artistic sensibility.

When I was young, I didn't know I was queer. I just thought I was an artist or a writer, or maybe just a sensitive soul. Being drawn to the things that assigned male children weren't supposed to be into.

There was so much flair in songleading. I can almost recall whispers about the more flamboyant songleaders. These traits were often comfortably overlooked because of how good they were at leading the singing. Just as long as they didn't have too much sugar in their tank.

My heart is so full when I'm harmonizing with hundreds of voices, singing songs we all know and have sung for decades, centuries even. I want to pluck that part completely out of the church tradition, but to me it isn't possible. It's a paradox, though. To get the best singing, in my experience, you might have to sit in the pews next to some bigots.

❧

Sometimes I wonder, what are the hymns of Appalachia?

We could pilfer through the Ken Burns country music documentary. Cycle between newgrass, bluegrass, Dolly Parton, Loretta Lynn, the Carter Family, and have to make a detour through "Wagon Wheel" or "Take Me Home, Country Roads." I'm no Appalachian musicologist or bluegrass aficionado, but I definitely know the feeling of the hymns of our region when I hear them. I know the peace that overwhelms me. The slightly crooked twang, softer than the country pop rock of the big city lights of Nashville. I know "Blue Moon of Kentucky" will keep me shining even though I'm a child of East Tennessee. And "Rocky Top" still gets my foot stomping and my hands clapping. I hear Rhiannon Giddens's banjo fly, Gillian Welch's glorious longing and sadness, Tyler Childers's sweet high mountain pitch, Amythyst Kiah's bluesy country soul.

It's not a hymnal or a playlist, it's just a sound. The same sound over and over. And I could listen to that sound, that hymn, for the rest of my life. And I certainly will.

To be queer and Appalachian is an imaginative choice. One that finds you singing a tune that may sound out of place to those outside of the region of your experience. But we sing the mountains here. We sing the hollers. We sing the cities. We sing a way of life that is hard fought. A paradox of identity. Constantly in flux. We sing the mountaintop removal. We sing the tree sits and blockades. We sing in nature. We sing in protest. We sing in inextricably complicated ways because sometimes that's all we have. Our voice. And we know how we have been silenced. We know how we will continue to be silenced. But we sing anyway.

No . . . Appalachia is not a mission field.

Although people have done their best to make it out to be. It's a place that knows what it is. And accepts us all. As we bring our hymns and queerness and fullest of selfs to reside in its belly. What's hard about Appalachia is what people have imagined it to be. They've imagined it to be a place where a person like me shouldn't belong. But people have been trying to change that ever since it was called Appalachia. And let me tell you it ain't going nowhere. I hear its song. I'm a member of the church of Appalachia. And everything I carried before, all the religious trauma, just washes away. Yeah, I fight to be here, for the spirit of what's already hovering over the mountains. What calls any of us here. A place to simply be. And rest in the energy of the nature and the sound. The same sound. A joyful chord. To be at rest.

Let us sing.

Scraps

Eileen Elizabeth Espinoza

To be queer is to make a life out of scraps.

⊱ ❦ ⊰

I say to the ocean: *bless us.*

The tide carries my prayers and you might catch them.

I pray for love.

⊱ ❦ ⊰

The shore was picked clean to the bone by the bathers and the waves. Shaw's Cove has a strict policy against collecting, but every trip I took one small shell, for J: a mussel, sucked out clean, and polished by the waves scraping against sand.

My vigil: wading through the tidepools, wandering the cliffs. The liminal space between the end and the beginning—

⊱ ❦ ⊰

This morning I tied up my long skirt into a makeshift dress. I touched an orange sea star, sunning itself in a perfect stretch between the rocks. I knelt to see the little school of fish go by and the red crabs scuttling along a long crevasse, settling into their kindergarten before the reef. A few heliotrope urchins glowed at the bottom of the clear pools. And the shy, seashell-covered anemone—

—did you know they cover themselves in broken seashells for sunblock?

—the anemone closed at my touch.

I am an Appalachian woman far from home, in the desert of California, looking for scraps.

❧

I am thinking of Emily Dickinson and the way she made a life of scraps—poems on the backs of envelopes and receipts and odd bits of paper; recycled fibers to make language.

—And did you know she kept the sabbath in the small rooms of her father's house? Her church was an apple orchard, her congregation were bees.

And her love was an envelope, receipts of their desire kept under her bone white laundry.

Still it was enough to make a life [of scraps] and record it on scraps, and to punctuate it with scraps—dashes short and long, like a letter cutter ripping away the tongue from the page. Emily [only] had the bees.

❧

To be queer is to make a life out of scraps.

❧

For the last three years I loved her [J] with such a burning.

We fell in love during the worst years of our lives—when everyone around us died, or tried to die, or otherwise left:

And we fell away from the old world, together.

We have survived so much already. Sunlight sears through me like stained glass, bleeding out color, and I consider how little elegance seems to remain in this dying world.

How much bracing beauty is left, if I can be soft enough to receive it?

When I hold the face of the woman I love, I want more than just the scraps of life. I want more than the bones.
I want to be seen, by the world, as a whole and worthy being—as someone deserving of love.

In November, we drove into the desert and watched the sky fade into night. I walked J to the best cluster of Joshua trees and started crying before I could even settle into the sand. I wrapped a silver moon around her neck and asked her to be my wife.

Do you know what it is like to feast on love after a lifetime of emotional famine?

I married her so that she didn't slip through my hands into another world.

My wife is a poet. My wife is trans. My wife believes in a kinder world than me, though she hasn't met it yet.

I move through this world in a body I have almost always loved; she moves in a body shifting, softening—almost loved. And then I hold her body and she is absolutely loved.

We have made a world of our love. It is a small world: the cove, our mountain, the desert, our cat, our dog. But it is a kind one.

If language is an incantation, then let me speak this:
I will take more than the scraps left behind for us. I will carry the bones.

Gathered in Hidden Valley in Joshua Tree National Park, and Jennifer and I married.

On our wedding night, after J fell asleep, I went to the sliding glass door of our Airbnb. I stood on the threshold of the glass door. I watched a single shooting star sail across the inky sky. I wished for a kinder world.

All that is left of Sappho are scraps. I wrote about this once:

> Perhaps what daunts and excites us most about Sappho's work are the gaps between words. The fragments thrill; they give us the experience of reading a papyrus. But more than anything, we can project ourselves in the void between her verses; we can position her lyrics to suit our own aesthetic needs and intellectual interpretations,

much how we would do with a song today. With her words, we can paint a fractured portrait of a woman two thousand years ago, but the portrait is like a sieve, catching our desires and letting her own words drip through.

⊰ ❦ ⊱

Yesterday, we brought our dog to Shaw's Cove. I think it was the first time she had seen the ocean. It was the first time we had come back to the shore since our wedding.

Our dog, a massive golden brown wolf dog called Freja, sat in the sand at J's feet, staring into the calm waves. Maybe it was something about the looming lunar eclipse to come, but the sea was completely, eerily, still.

On that shore I watched the world through three sets of eyes—hers, mine, and our marriage's. How comfortably this third conscience has slipped around us, like a string of moons around a planet. A ring.

⊰ ❦ ⊱

"And her light
stretches over salt sea
equally and flowerdeep fields." —Sappho

⊰ ❦ ⊱

J and I live tucked away from the world, at the mouth of a wilderness trail. Each day I can look out from our bedroom window to the Box Spring Mountains, where donkeys cry out in the afternoons and gaunt coyotes trot through our yard at night. It is an overlooked scrap of land—a paradise, our sun-scorched earth, a smudge on the map. It is holy land.

In the evenings we sit in our beach chairs in the yard and watch two pairs of birds: one set of ravens, and the other, some small songbirds. One raven waits on the power line, every dusk, for its mate. On the cable below, a songbird waits. We watch the day break and the birds come.

Most mornings, I look for quail. From my east-facing windows, I watch the sagebrush for their plump feathered bodies, waiting for them to dart into my scrub lawn. I watch how they tend low to the earth to forage for their seeds, how their topknot of feathers bounces with their upright jolts. When they run, each clump of feathers is a quiet sail.

I'm a queer Appalachian. I live in a world that wants my wife to die. I live in a place that only newly legalized my marriage to her. I live in a place that routinely tries to legislate us out of existence.

Families like ours have to plan for the end of justice. We cannot trust our government to protect us. We can count on our government to harm us.

Every morning we fight the urge to read the latest proposed legislation that would strip her of her humanity. We read the news and we must do two things: make a plan for how to stay, and make a plan for how to leave.

To be queer and trans in America is to fight for leftover scraps. But to be trans in America is to be forgotten.

If my words can become a spell, I cast one of protection around her. A ring.

Several days into a dissociative fugue, I opened the front door of my house to a pale blue morning. Desert quail softly darted from their grazing. One lingered. The lookout. A dark gray thing, with careful movements. He watched me, and I watched him back.

On the perimeter of the land I rent, smoke trees stand gray and tall like ghosts. That morning, I raked my hands across the fallen branches and sandy soil, filling my fingernails with earth. I carved out a dip under the low branches, pulling myself under the shade of the tree. Sheltered from the morning sun, I watched the birds move through the brush and over the berm into the foothills, until I fell asleep.

I listen for the quail. We do not die.

A few nights ago, as we pulled our car into the garage, a quail from the covey in our yard flew into the door. One of Chopin's nocturnes was still playing as we stepped out of the car into the fading light to see what happened. I knelt to the ground and held its dark round body in my hands as it died. I felt the heat slowly leave its body, rising into the night. The comma of its head feathers became a question mark.

I raked my hands across the fallen branches and sandy soil, filling my fingernails with earth. I carved out a dip under the low branches. I left him there to rest.

I prayed for love.

❧

Our wedding ceremony was brief— perhaps an hour—standing in the desert with our chosen family and friends. From a green notebook she gifted me on my twenty-ninth birthday, I read my vows:

> J—
>
> We are standing in what used to be an ocean. The sand and rocks around us are as old as time herself. This cathedral of the desert has been slowly carved away by millennia of winds and sunshine. It stands today as our little church of wilderness—a testament to the union of sand and wind.
>
> In this desert, our desert, we have conjured an ancient love. A holy love.
>
> I have heard that a marriage ends when one of the pair dies. But this will not be the case for us. I will love you in every life after this one—
>
> When my body rejoins the Earth in the slow dance of sand and soil merging to make the next climbing boulders, when the water of my body rises from me to fall again as rain upon the ocean—I will love you as the yucca moth loves the Joshua tree and follow you the way the river follows the pull of the tide under our perfect moon.
>
> Under these stars, I prayed for love.

> And so in the company of our loved ones and this great wilderness, I promise to love you for every day of my life, and for every ocean and desert that comes after—until you and I are rejoined as the dust that makes desert cathedrals, or stars.

❧

I am thinking of Emily Dickinson and the way she made a life of scraps—a religion of scraps—

poems on the backs of envelopes and receipts and odd bits of paper, recycled fibers to make language. And she kept the sabbath in small rooms. Her church was an apple orchard, a congregation of bees.

Still it was enough to make a life [of scraps] and record it on scraps, and to punctuate it with scraps—dashes short and long, like a letter cutter ripping away the tongue from the page—

Emily had the bees.

❧

To be queer is to make a life out of scraps.

❧

As dearly as we desire, we may never have a child together. But we will always have life around us to care for, however briefly. There are tide pools to wade in and quail to watch, and desert skies to sleep under.

And we have the small world that we have made together, in the space between our bodies. our heat, our language, our dirt.

Every morning the soft desert light illuminates J's gentle face—and the soft animal of my body isn't always feral—it also knows how to love.

Contributors

Chelsea Bock (she/her/hers) is an enrollment services staff member and adjunct English and communications instructor at Anne Arundel Community College near Annapolis, Maryland. She is currently working on her educational doctorate at Rockhurst University with a research focus in LGBTQ+ student support. When she's not writing, teaching, or learning, she enjoys roller skating, dancing to '80s music, building Legos, and spending time with her husband and their cat.

Willie Edward Taylor Carver Jr. (any pronouns) is an Appalachian author, advocate, educator, and past Kentucky Teacher of the Year. His writing has appeared in a number of publications, including *Appalachian Journal*, *The Louisville Review*, *Southern Humanities*, *Good River Review*, and *Salvation South*. His debut collection, *Gay Poems for Red States*, was featured on *Good Morning America* and was named a Book Riot Best Book, a Top Ten Over the Rainbow Book by the American Library Association, and a Whippoorwill Honor Book; it also received a Stonewall Honor award. He lives with his husband and three cats in rural Kentucky.

Emma Cieslik (she/her) is a queer, disabled, and neurodivergent religious scholar and museum worker based in Washington. She researches the intersections of gender, sexuality, religion, and material culture. She runs Queer and Catholic: A CLGS Oral History Project, focused on documenting stories of trauma alongside liberation and queer joy.

Eileen Elizabeth Espinoza (she/her) is a queer Appalachian poet, essayist, and professor living in the California redwoods. She cofounded *Boshemia*, a British American arts and culture magazine published in the UK. She is the recipient of the 2021 McQuern Award in Nonfiction, a finalist for the 2021 Annie Dillard Award for Creative Nonfiction, and a finalist for the 2020 Marica and Jan Vilcek Prize for Poetry. Her nonfiction appears in the *Los Angeles Review of Books*, *Bellevue Literary Review*, *Joyland Magazine*, and elsewhere. Her first book, *Carrying the Bones: Rituals for a Dying World* (University Press of Kentucky, 2026), explores the social and sacred function of grief rituals in the West.

John Golden (he/they) is a washed-out engineer, a seminary graduate, an aspiring minister, a queer Tex-Appalachian, and a proud member of the Presbyterian Church (USA). John has worked for a Presbyterian Campus Ministry in East Tennessee and strives to build communities of faith, hope, love, and witness that welcome people from the entire spectrum of gender and sexual identity diversity.

Matthew Jacobson (he/him) is from Huntington, West Virginia, and prefers his hot dogs with sauce and slaw. After graduating high school in Cincinnati, he attended Saint Louis University and graduated with a BA in Theological Studies. There, in the spring of 1998, he met his husband, Brian, at ye olde gay bar. Matthew is a chaplain and received his Master's of Divinity from Loyola University of Chicago. He is board certified with the National Association of Catholic Chaplains and has served as a palliative care chaplain at West Virginia University Medicine in Morgantown; Northwestern Memorial Hospital in Chicago; and Rhode Island and Hasbro Children's Hospitals in Providence. He continues his service as the palliative care chaplain at Johns Hopkins Bayview Medical Center in Baltimore. He lives in Maryland with Brian and their children. Storytelling, silence, hiking, singing out loud, cooking, gardening, Psalm 121, and stargazing are his favorite forms of prayer.

Jarred Johnson (he/they) grew up on a farm in the Appalachian foothills outside Somerset, Kentucky. He received his MFA in fiction from UNC Wilmington, where he taught creative writing and was on staff at *Ecotone Magazine*. His work has appeared in *Oxford American*, *Bat City Review*, and *Baltimore Review*, and he has received grants from the Fulbright Program and the German Academic Exchange Service. Jarred lives in Nashville where they're finishing a novel about virtual reality and the end of coal mining.

Raychel Kool (they/them) is a queer and trans hillbilly creative from Adena, Hopewell, Myaamia, Osage, Shawnee, and Cherokee lands in the hills of rural Kentucky. They currently live on Tiwa lands in Albuquerque, New Mexico. They recently graduated from the University of New Mexico, where they served as an editor for the literary magazines *Scribendi* and *Conceptions Southwest*. They're also a part of the Stay Together Appalachian Youth (STAY) Project. Raychel is a big fan of zines, sun tea, and porch sittin'.

Julie Rae Powers (she/they) is from West Virginia and Virginia. They come from a working-class family of homemakers, teachers, coal miners, and railroad laborers. Their photographic and written work has focused on family history, coal, Appalachia, and queerness. Additionally, they are the author and editor of a forthcoming collection of Queer Appalachian photographers, *Reclamation: Queering Appalachia's Visual History* (University Press of Kentucky) and a collection of personal essays, *To Thine Own Self Be True* (University Press of Kentucky).

Mack Rogers (he/they) is a queer Black writer whose work appears in *Foglifter*, *The Offing*, *Shenandoah*, and elsewhere. Mack is a staff critic for *Pencilhouse*, poetry reader at *Split Lip Magazine*, and poetry editor for *Zero Readers Magazine*. His debut chapbook, *Hindsight*, published with Diode Editions, released in March 2025. He lives with his partner and their three cats in Raleigh, North Carolina.

Davis Shoulders (any pronouns) is a queer Appalachian bookseller and writer based in Hazard, Kentucky. They are a series editor for the University Press of Kentucky's *Appalachian Futures: Black, Native, & Queer Voices*; this essay collection is the first project under their purview since its inception in 2020. Davis also has a forthcoming memoir from University Press of Kentucky about their experience growing up as a preacher's kid in the Churches of Christ and their continued mystical exploration beyond that faith tradition. They enjoy a nice walk, a gentle conversation, and creating "stick art" and would love to give you a tarot reading if you are ever in the mood.

Savannah Sipple (she/her) is a writer and editor from Kentucky. Her first book, *WWJD and Other Poems* (Sibling Rivalry, 2019), was included on the American Library Association's Over the Rainbow Recommended LGBTQ Reading List. It explores what it is to be a queer woman in Appalachia and is rooted in its culture and in her body. Savannah is also a special projects editor at *GO Magazine*, and she's currently working on both a novel and a memoir. Savannah resides in Lexington with her wife.

Joe Tolbert Jr. (he/him) is a writer and cultural organizer who works at the intersections of art and culture, spirituality, and collective liberation. He received his BS in Communications from the University of Tennessee, Knoxville, and completed his MDiv in Social Ethics at Union Theological Seminary in the city of New York. He is a sought-after facilitator, creative producer, and cultural strategist who works with communities and arts institutions to help them harness the power of art and culture through his company, Art at the Intersections.

APPALACHIAN FUTURES
Black, Native, and Queer Voices

SERIES EDITORS: Annette Saunooke Clapsaddle, Davis Shoulders, and Crystal Wilkinson

This book series gives voice to Black, Native, Latinx, Asian, Queer, and other nonwhite or ignored identities within the Appalachian region.

Black Freedom Struggle in Urban Appalachia
Edited by J. Z. Bennett, Christy L. McGuire, Lori Delale-O'Connor, T. Elon Dancy II, and Sabina Vaught

Affrilachia: Testimonies
Chris Aluka Berry with Kelly Elaine Navies and Maia A. Surdam

Teresa Martín & Luisa Menéndez: Indigenous Women from Appalachia in the Spanish Colonial Record
Edited by Melissa D. Birkhofer and Paul M. Worley

No Son of Mine: A Memoir
Jonathan Corcoran

To Belong Here: A New Generation of Queer, Trans, and Two-Spirit Appalachian Writers
Edited by Rae Garringer

Tar Hollow Trans: Essays
Stacy Jane Grover

Nobody's Psychic: Finding & Losing Yourself
Dani Lamorte

Deviant Hollers: Queering Appalachian Ecologies for a Sustainable Future
Edited by Zane McNeill and Rebecca Scott

Reading, Writing, and Queer Survival: Affects, Matterings, and Literacies Across Appalachia
Caleb Pendygraft

Queer Communion: Religion in Appalachia
Edited by Davis Shoulders

Appalachian Ghost: A Photographic Reimagining of the Hawk's Nest Tunnel Disaster
Raymond Thompson Jr.